The
Promises
of
Grace

The Promises of Grace

Living in the Grip of God's Love

Bryan Chapell

 Baker Books

A Division of Baker Book House Co
Grand Rapids, Michigan 49516

Published by Baker Books
a division of Baker Book House Company
P.O. Box 6287, Grand Rapids, MI 49516–6287

Printed in the United States of America

Library of Congress Cataloging-in-Publication Data

Chapell, Bryan.
    [In the grip of grace]
    The promises of grace: living in the grip of God's love / Bryan Chapell.
       p.   cm.
    Previously published in 1992.
    ISBN 0-8010-6370-1 (pbk.)
    1. Bible. N. T. Romans VIII—Meditations. I. Title.
BS2665.54.C47 2001
227′.106—dc21
                                     00-054717

Names of individuals and occasional specifics are changed in some personal accounts appearing in this book to respect the concerns and wishes of those involved. My debt is great to those who have taught me the gospel of grace with the testimony of their lives.

For current information about all releases from Baker Book House, visit our web site: http://www.bakerbooks.com

Contents

INTRODUCTION

The Promises of Grace

"Come See Live Pheasant!" "Come Pet Baby Pigs!" "Come See Live Buffalo!" The series of billboards beckoned us to veer off the highway to get our gas and a meal at "Cowboy Bob's Circus of Fun."

Somehow Cowboy Bob seemed to know that it would take more than cheap gasoline prices and a hamburger to get vacationers off the interstate. So, as we neared his exit, each billboard made bigger and more exotic promises. Not only could we pet baby pigs, but soon, we learned, we could "Feed Live Rattlesnakes" (we hoped not with the baby pigs). But the best attractions were yet to come. "Come see the five-legged cow," the next billboard advertised. And if that were not tantalizing enough, then the "six-legged steer" touted on the next sign was sure to allure. Yet to come, however, was the promise of all promises—the biggest and best, saved for last. Lest we even think about driving by Cowboy Bob's without a visit, the final billboard

promised we could see "THE WORLD'S LARGEST ARMADILLO."
Who could resist a promise like that?

Promises have power. It is the reason we want to use
them. Promises have the power to persuade, to assure, and
to attract. Promises have so much power that we are
tempted to use bigger and better promises to manipulate
others. As a result, promises tend to get out of hand. A
rundown store in central Kansas attracts customers with
billboard promises of "New and Old Antiques"—a questionable promise, to say the least, but no more questionable than the promises Christians sometimes make to
attract others to God.

Christians so much want others to accept Jesus Christ
as Lord and Savior, we are tempted to sell Jesus on the billboard of the big promise: "Accept Jesus as your Savior,
and God will grant you business success"; "Trust in Jesus,
and you will never get sick again"; "Turn your life over to
Jesus, and all your problems will disappear." The promises are not always so bold, not always so self-serving, but
all of us recognize their allure.

We want to be able to tell others that when Jesus enters
their lives, fantastic things happen. We tell them that salvation is free, but somehow we know they will not accept
it simply because it is cheap. We want to be able to promise something wonderful.

But what does God promise? If the godly are supposed
to be wealthy, then why was Jesus poor? If holiness assures
health, then why did all the apostles die? If being in God's
family wipes away all problems, then why did Mary and
Martha argue?

Whenever we try to define God's promises in terms of
this world's benefits, faith seems foolish. The reason is
God does not promise us the benefits of this world. God
says he has "chosen those who are poor in the eyes of the
world to be rich in faith" (James 2:5). Jesus said, "My kingdom is not of this world" (John 18:36). Because of these

truths you may think God's promises are of no earthly good. Or you can believe a wonderful alternative: God makes bigger and better promises that are "out of this world" (although they may be experienced here).

What does God really promise? Over four hundred years ago some courageous saints of the English Reformation tried to answer that question for believers who would suffer great loss and persecution. A great temptation then was to promote the Christianity of the big promise, to offer assurances of easier times and more prosperous futures. But these Reformers knew that Jesus had urged his followers not to put their hopes in "treasures on earth, where moth and rust destroy, and where thieves break in and steal" (Matt. 6:19).

Jesus taught that what is really important and assures joy and peace in a world corrupted by sin is not found in physical prosperity but in spiritual security: God promised grace. The benefits of God's grace are so overwhelming, so sure, and so powerful that they defy the ability of the troubles of this world to dampen our faith or spoil our joy.

The Reformers wrote what they believed about God's goodness in covenants, confessions, catechisms, and other documents. In these they frequently divided God's present work of grace into three categories: justification, adoption, and sanctification. Often Christians still use these categories to describe God's grace. Justification is God's gracious forgiving of believers' sins solely because Jesus suffered and died for them (1 Peter 2:23–25). Adoption is God's gracious act of making believers in Christ part of his family, because they are now clothed in the righteousness of his Son (John 1:12–13). Sanctification is God's gracious work of making believers more like Jesus Christ by the work of his Holy Spirit in their lives (Rom. 8:9–11). Each of these aspects of God's grace flows into the life of every true believer. They are like fountains of blessing that pour out the benefits God guarantees.

The classic expressions of these benefits now may seem somewhat archaic and are unfamiliar to many, but they capture the beauty of God's grace with an endearing simplicity from which we can still learn. What are the wonderful things God promises believers? The writers of the *Westminster Catechism* answered this way:

> The benefits which in this life accompany or flow from justification, adoption and sanctification include:
> assurance of God's love,
> peace of conscience,
> joy in the Holy Ghost,
> increase of grace,
> and perseverance therein to the end.

These five beautiful benefits are the real promises of God for believers' lives today, and they undergird the thoughts in this book. The wording of these authors may not be perfect in every respect, but it focuses believers' expectations on the promises they really can expect God to fulfill in this life.

God does not promise every believer more money and fewer headaches. God promises confidence of our relationship with him. If God wanted to promise us easy street, he would not have commanded us to take up our crosses daily. Oh sure, God may grant material blessings, long lives, and united families. Sometimes we pray for such blessings, and God answers in the way he knows is best. But the real benefits of grace are not a new Lexus, skin that does not wrinkle, and a family that never gets out of sorts. If these were the benefits all Christians were to expect, most of us would consider ourselves shortchanged. The benefits God promises to all believers are not that worldly and not that fragile.

Christians whose joy is full have discovered happiness in what this world cannot offer and cannot deny.

The promises of grace are not recorded in a bankbook, they do not rely on a doctor's diagnosis, and difficulty cannot erase them. This book is devoted to reminding everyone to cherish the real promises of grace. By focusing on the genuine benefits of grace, Christians can rediscover the promises God designed to make their lives more satisfying and less selfish, more fulfilling and less driven, more peaceful and less guilt ridden.

This book will take you through only one chapter of the Bible: Romans 8. The truths there are so remarkable and so encouraging, you will find yourself visiting God again and again in its passages. The trip through this Scripture will be no detour, for this journey does not advertise the Christianity of the big promise. It promises to reveal the goodness of grace for everyday life. Come, enjoy the promises of grace.

QUESTIONS *for Thought*

1. Why are Christians tempted to "sell" the gospel with big promises of this world's goods and gain?
2. What types of promises do Christians sometimes use to lure others to faith in Jesus Christ?
3. What is wrong with promising that Jesus will put an end to all a person's troubles and trials in this life?
4. What does God really promise?
5. How can you benefit from the promises of God today?

PART ONE

Calming Storms

ONE

No Condemnation

One cold January on a cliff in Missouri my brother Gordon scared some peace into me. He was on a holiday leave from the Air Force and visited me at college to help relieve my winter doldrums. Promising to teach me mountain climbing "in one easy lesson," he shoved me into my old Chrysler, and we headed for the Missouri mountains.

Our destination was a set of cliffs above the Black River in the foothills of the Ozarks. I began to get a true picture of what was in store for me, however, only when we were about halfway there. That was when this brother told me another brother had ducked out of this adventure because his wife had declared it too dangerous for "a family man."

"What are you getting me into?" I gulped.

"Don't get excited," Gordon said. "I know what I'm doing."

For the moment that answer was enough. I calmed the queasiness in my stomach with mental reminders that my brother is a highly trained rescue specialist. I reasoned, *Gordon has conducted rescue missions all over the world, in every imaginable terrain and climate. Surely he can take care of me in Missouri. If he says he can teach me to rappel down a mountain, I have nothing to be worried about.* "No sweat," he said. *No problem,* I thought.

It was easy at first. We went to some gently sloping bluffs that I backed down using the rappel rope. I learned how to put proper tension on the rope to adjust the speed of my descent. No problem! But then it was time to graduate.

We climbed above the rushing, rock-strewn river to the highest cliff in sight. This cliff did not slope; it sliced "backward" away from its edge. To go off this cliff was to go off into nothing but thin air. "No problem," I thought. "I now know how to rappel. I have learned from the best."

I started backing off the cliff into one hundred feet of nothing but air, when the diameter of that rope suddenly caught my eye. Gordon had told me it was specially made, high-quality, superstrength climbing rope; but that line on which my life now depended was only about a half-inch thick. I was going to jump off a cliff, and this "thread" was supposed to hold me. My heart began thumping in my throat. My hands were suddenly clammy, and my knees felt as if they were filled with Jell-O.

I was so scared I was nearly paralyzed. But I did not want to show I was afraid. After all, there was my brother looking on and grinning like a cat who had just cornered a canary. Still, I was having a little trouble making my knees work as I backed slowly off the precipice. That is probably why I slipped. Off the cliff I fell like a stone—for about three feet. Then the rope caught me, pulled taut, and I hung suspended above the rocky river. Blood pounded in my ears like fireworks exploding, my breathing sounded like a runaway steam engine, and my eyes darted back and forth in panicked questioning from the rocks below to the rope above. But I hung there. The rope held me. It didn't break. I didn't fall.

Gradually, as I realized that amazing rope would not break, I relaxed. My heart slowed down. My breathing became regular. I actually began to enjoy the view. Somehow being in such great danger and yet so secure created a calmness—a sense of such overwhelming peace—that the tranquility of that moment is etched in my memory.

The Security of God's Love

In Romans 8 the apostle Paul shows believers God's love is like that rappeller's rope. It will not break despite the pressures put on it by a slip into sin, the collapse of circumstances, or a fall arranged by Satan. God's love will hold against these pressures that we might think would put our souls in eternal danger. Nothing can separate us from the love of God that is in Christ Jesus our Lord, says the apostle as this chapter concludes (vv. 38–39). But here in the opening verses of the chapter a derivative truth beacons: If God's love will never, never fail, what is the result of a Christian's being in such great danger while being so secure? Peace!

The overwhelming peace that is ours as a result of the security God provides is Paul's theme as this great Bible passage begins. But the theme is more than an introduction to a passage, it is the confirmation of a promise of God to all believers in Christ Jesus. The first promise Paul urges us to claim that will calm our fears and ease our hearts is *peace of conscience.*

Romans 8:1–16

¹Therefore, there is now no condemnation for those who are in Christ Jesus, ²because through Christ Jesus the law of the Spirit of life set me free from the law of sin and death. ³For what the law was powerless to do in that it was weakened by the sinful nature, God did by sending his own Son in the likeness of sinful man to be a sin offering. And so he condemned sin in sinful man, ⁴in order that the righteous requirements of the law might be fully met in us, who do not live according to the sinful nature but according to the Spirit.

⁵Those who live according to the sinful nature have their minds set on what that nature desires; but those who live in accordance with the Spirit have their minds set on what the Spirit desires. ⁶The mind of sinful man is death, but the mind controlled by the Spirit is life and peace, ⁷because the sinful mind is hostile to God. It does not submit to God's law, nor can it do so. ⁸Those controlled by the sinful nature cannot please God.

⁹You, however, are controlled not by the sinful nature but by the Spirit, if the Spirit of God lives in you. And if anyone does not have the Spirit of Christ, he does not belong to Christ. ¹⁰But if Christ is in you, your body is dead because of sin, yet your spirit is alive because of righteousness. ¹¹And if the Spirit of him who raised Jesus from the dead is living in you, he who raised Christ from the dead will also give life to your mortal bodies through his Spirit, who lives in you.

¹²Therefore, brothers, we have an obligation—but it is not to the sinful nature, to live according to it. ¹³For if you live according to the sinful nature, you will die; but if by the Spirit you put to death the misdeeds of the body, you will live, ¹⁴because those who are led by the Spirit of God are sons of God. ¹⁵For you did not receive a spirit that makes you a slave again to fear, but you received the Spirit of sonship. And by him we cry, "*Abba*, Father." ¹⁶The Spirit himself testifies with our spirit that we are God's children.

The Storms of Conscience

"I am a freak." The words were said with anger, fists clenched, eyes toward heaven. Then the young man dropped his head and began to sob in desperation and agony. The pastor listening to the tormented confession had been looking for him for two days. This self-professed "freak" had been a Christian leader in his city, but over the last year innumerable difficulties had pressed him to a breaking point. He was in trouble on every front—family, business, church. Beyond reasonable thought and seeking some release—some outlet for pent-up frustration and desperation—he had fled to a liaison with a former lover. Not surprisingly, the pressures did not ease with this attempt at relief.

Two days after the liaison, only a week after this father of two learned that his wife was expecting twins, he was fired from his job. Then the pressure was too much. He ran. He cleaned out the family bank accounts of what little money there was, took the family car, and left town by himself. He abandoned his family.

Over the next two days the pastor drove around the young man's former hangouts looking for some sign of him. Once he caught a glimpse of the young man at an intersection, but the man saw the pastor and bolted, running a red light. After another day of looking the pastor had to give up. He was driving home from a church meeting in a neighboring town when he saw the car of the young man parked at a fast-food restaurant. The pastor drove his car directly behind the parked car, blocking it into its parking place.

The young man was eating in the car, but when the pastor walked to his door, the man would not even look up. He did not talk. He did not move. The pastor said, "Jim, I've come to take you home." There was no response. The pastor tried again, "Jim, I'll take you to my home." Still the young man's eyes remained in a fixed stare at the dashboard. He was as a man paralyzed. It was not as though he was resisting the suggestions but as though he was beyond resistance. He seemed drained of energy and nearly lifeless—more a corpse than a rebel.

The pastor opened Jim's car door, took his arm, helped him to his feet, and steered him to the other car. The young man walked like a rag doll. His wobbly legs seemed almost unable to support his weight at times. When they reached the passenger door, Jim would not even lift his arm to press the latch. The pastor opened the door and half steered, half lifted Jim into the car. When they reached the pastor's home, the whole process was repeated in reverse.

The pastor took Jim to the spare room that doubled as an office, and it was there that frustration turned from limp resignation to angry defiance. The young man clenched his fists and shouted, "I am a freak."

The words burst from Jim in a torrent of bitter tears: "I am a freak. I am supposed to be a Christian leader in this community. I am supposed to lead others to Christ. But I do what I hate. I can't control my own body. I even ran out on my family. I am hopeless, hopeless! Why did God make me this way? Why does he tolerate me? How can he love me after this? I am a freak. I am a freak."

I tell you now of this soul in torment not for your pity and not for your condemnation. I tell you of this young man, still loved by many Christians, including me, to remind us all of the anguish Christians face when they fall into terrible sin. This man's words and actions exemplify the storms of conscience that buffet their hearts when temptation overwhelms them. The storms of conscience that assault their peace, and echo in this young man's cries, are easily recognized. In the wake of his sin he says, in essence, "I am not good, I am not strong, I cannot be God's."

I know these storms of conscience. You do. They are the storms that always rage against God's peace in our hearts when we sin. Our sin may not be the same sort as this young man's, but our guilt can be just as troubling. Still, despite the destructive potential of these storms, God promises peace to his people. How can this be? How can people assaulted by sin's guilt know God's peace? What can be done to quiet the storms in others' consciences, or in our own?

For answers we must turn to the One who faced another storm and calmed it by the power of his word. When Jesus said, "Peace, be still," the wind and waves ceased. His Word yet has the power to still storms, even the storms of conscience. Against a raging storm of guilt, God calls out the promise of forgiveness in this passage of his Word, saying again, "Peace, be still." If we are to claim the peace God promises, we must confront the storms of conscience with this Word of God—the Word that whispers grace and brings peace. Even a heart storm can be calmed by the words of a Savior who yet says, "Peace, be still."

Calming the Storm of Self-Blame

The first storm of conscience that we must confront with the Word of God is characterized in Jim's words of self-condemnation: "I am sinful, a freak." His conscience cries, "I am not good." This is the storm of self-blame. Into the teeth of the storm that howls "I am not good," we must cast the words the apostle Paul writes at the beginning of Romans 8: "There is now no condemnation for those who are in Christ Jesus" (v. 1).

There is no condemnation for those who are Christ's. The words of the apostle are carefully chosen for us who would know and communicate God's peace. Note the Word of God does *not* say, "There is now no sin"; nor,

"If you are in Christ, you will not now sin"; nor yet, "If you happen to sin now, nothing is really wrong." Such words would fly in the face of other Scripture and the true feelings of believers whose consciences are convicted of sin.

Yet, despite the fact that God says nothing to deny the seriousness of sin, often our first tendency in speaking to ourselves or to other believers who are troubled by personal sin is to belittle the sin. We say, "Oh, don't get so upset. It's not so bad. Everybody makes mistakes. There's nothing really wrong." We tell ourselves or others to be at peace, because the sin is not so serious. But when a storm of conscience rages, these words mean nothing. They may cause people to ignore the waves for a while, but that will only get them in deeper trouble. God's approach is far different. He never tells anyone to ignore the storm or make light of the sin.

Broadcast Grace

The Word of God does not say there is no sin, but that there is no condemnation. Paul minces no words about the seriousness of sin. He says:

> [2]Through Christ Jesus the law of the Spirit of life set me free from the law of sin and death. [3]For what the law was powerless to do in that it was weakened by the sinful nature, God did by sending his own Son in the likeness of sinful man to be a sin offering. And so he condemned sin in sinful man.

God condemns sin. He does not regard it lightly. In fact, sin is so serious, it carries with it a death penalty. The "law of sin and death" to which Paul refers here is explained in the preceding chapter (see Rom. 7:10–11). There Paul says that because of sin he was too weak to keep the law, which was designed to keep him in a living union with God. As a result, the law was powerless to maintain his life with God and actually condemned him. Since he could not do what the law required to keep his relationship with God alive, each standard became a death verdict against him. The situation would be hopeless except for what God did because of the seriousness of sin.

God sent his own Son as a sin offering to meet the requirements of the law for us. In the Old Testament the people of God sacrificed unblemished animals as sin offerings to indicate the guilt of their sin. The death of the sacrificed animal symbolized the seriousness of the sin even as it indicated God's willingness to put the penalty of breaking his law on another. God graciously allowed the sacrifice of an animal to satisfy his justice. He kept a living union with his people even though they did not keep his holy law.

What God symbolized with an innocent animal he fulfilled with the innocent blood of his Son. An animal could never really pay the full penalty for sin. So God kept the living union with his people by providing his Son as the ultimate sin offering on the cross. Christ's death in one divine gesture indicates both how great is God's love and how terrible is sin. Sin in people and on them is so horrible that the life of Christ was required to pay its penalty.

No one should ever say his or her own sin is not serious. God believed it was so serious that the life of his own Son was required to pay its price. But even as God affirms the seriousness of sin by Christ's death, he broadcasts the hope sinners have through the cross. The full penalty for sin was paid on the cross. Yes, sin is horrible, but God provided a perfect offering to cancel its terrible guilt. So there is no condemnation for those who come to the cross. These truths of Scripture change Christians' efforts to find peace; instead of trying to belittle sin, they now claim the grace of God. God does not ask them to calm a storm of conscience by pretending it is not serious; he encourages them to confront it with a more powerful force. They are not to belittle the storm but to broadcast God's power over it.

Sometimes Christians are actually surprised to hear these truths. I have listened to Christians grieve over their sin saying, "Pastor, I am so awful, I am so sinful, I did this horrible, awful thing. I am so guilty." And I have watched their eyes fly wide open in horror when I have responded, "You're right. It is awful. You did wrong. It is terrible. I deny none of it. You are guilty." But the horrified eyes soon glisten with a deeper peace when I conclude, "So, take all of that guilt—no more and no less than what is all true—take it to the cross of Jesus and lay it down. Deny none of it. Confess it all for the horror it is. Put it before Jesus and let the grace of God wash it all away." There may be great sin, but there is now no condemnation to those who are in Christ Jesus. He has power of peace.

Butcher-Knife Lesson

One of the surprising things about ministry is to discover how many people, far into their adult years, live for the approval of their parents. Too many are constantly devastated, paralyzed, and spiritually weakened by knowing they will never truly receive that approval. Living with condemnation destroys. People change—truly calm their raging storms—when they finally realize there is no condemnation. Such a person is the young man whom I have called Jim in this chapter.

Jim was raised in rural Texas by a man pitiable in his own Christian understanding. As Jim was growing up, his family had Bible devotions, but they were hardly loving. The family had devotions whenever Jim's policeman father was drunk. When he came home from a drinking binge feeling guilty (whatever the time of day or night), he would gather the family, even if he had to awaken them from sleep.

He had the children sit in a circle on the living room floor. He stuck a butcher knife in the floor in front of them, threatening to use it on anyone who fell asleep. Then for hours he read from the Bible of the "grace" of God.

As Jim matured, his slight build, blond hair, and sensitive spirit increasingly irritated his father. Jim was not manly enough to satisfy the older man's expectations. After drinking too much one night, he confronted Jim with a pistol. Jim's father said he didn't want a "queer" (his father's word) for a son and began to shoot. Jim escaped only by jumping through a closed window.

From then on Jim was a failure in his father's eyes. It did not matter how often his sales topped the company chart or how fine a family he raised. Nothing removed his father's condemnation. Over the years the continual rejection and the constant reminder of his worthlessness in his father's eyes altered Jim. Doubts about his manhood depressed him, haunted him, weakened him. Affirmation of his manhood obsessed him and drove him to one sad relationship after another. He could not escape the condemnation, and as a result, he could not escape his sin. He would go for years free of the adultery, then the depression and guilt would rise with some tension or disappointment. He would seek an escape and sin again. Guilt controlled his actions for a while, but sooner or later this same guilt created enough self-doubt and pressure to weaken him and he fell again.

All of this was on his heart that night in the pastor's office when Jim cried out, "I am a freak, a freak." In that moment the minister did not know what to do, but he knew what was true. He said, "Jim, you're not a freak. You have been wrong, but God forgives. God forgives." With that the pastor embraced him.

Jim practically fell from the preacher's arms as the young businessman's knees gave way. Strength seemed to wash out of him. All that had been holding him up for years—

anger, public appearance, personal resolve—vanished when just one person who represented the gospel and knew the worst about him said, "Neither do I condemn you. There is now no condemnation for those in Christ Jesus."

Not everything suddenly became right in Jim's life as a result of those words that night. But this was the point of change when Jim's healing began. He no longer hid the depth of his sin from himself, but neither was his pardon hidden. As deep as was his sin, he knew deeper still was God's love. God said there is no condemnation to those who are in Christ Jesus. The sin Jim truly confessed was truly forgiven. That truth, more than all the guilt a conscience could muster and a parent could bestow, led to his real strength against temptation in spiritual health and peace.

Jim's story and the gospel of grace remind us how careful we believers must be not to slight the storms of conscience but to claim the peace of pardon. Many of us have not been the parents we should have been. We must not hide from our failings, but neither can we fail to remember that for those who are in Christ Jesus there is no condemnation. Many of us have not been as faithful to loved ones as we should have been. We should not deny or diminish the truth, because there is no condemnation for those who confess their sin and seek the Savior. Even if we have failed God in ways hidden to all but him, there is still no condemnation if we fully acknowledge the wrong before him.

Spiritual health never comes from belittling sin, but from a willingness to bathe its filthy entirety in the compassion of God. Our hearts will not be whole, nor will our lives be more holy, if every room and dark corner in them does not echo the promise, "There is now no condemnation." In God's pardon is the peace that enables us believers to face the sin that threatens us and part with the sin that batters us. The storm of self-blame dies when we hear the Savior say, "Peace, there is now no condemnation."

QUESTIONS
for Thought

1. How can it be that sinners would not be condemned by a holy God? Is there no condemnation for some because they are better than others?
2. What is the basis of the pardon that God extends to those he loves? What is its source? How is it claimed?
3. What are the limits of God's pardon? Are some sins greater than God's forgiveness?

TWO

Grace Whispers Peace

Even as the storm of self-blame is dying, there is another storm that may be gathering on the horizon. When my struggling friend Jim shook his fist at heaven, he not only said "I am not good," he also said, "I am not strong." Even though the past was forgiven and future sin would be forgiven, his conscience was tormented by the knowledge of his weakness. Jim felt worthless because he believed he was helpless against the forces that were such a powerful temptation in his life. Forgiveness did not clear his mind of the shame and the dread of his weakness. Self-doubt was the new storm with which he had to wrestle.

Calming the Storm of Self-Doubt

Most of us can identify with the storm of self-doubt that torments the conscience. When we fall into the temptation that has already grabbed us a hundred times, we are devastated as much by our sense of helplessness as we are by our sense of guilt. We recognize we have let ourselves, God, and perhaps others down in matters where we vowed we would not fail again. Our hearts cry out, "I know better, I knew better when I sinned. What is wrong with me? Even if God forgives me, I am so weak, I cannot be trusted. I don't trust myself. I am out of control. I can't stop even what I know is wrong." These words that surge from our hearts with gale force epitomize the storm of self-doubt. We agonize over our impotence in the face of sin, and the more we writhe in our weakness the stronger the storm seems to grow. God does not intend for such a storm to linger. The Bible teaches that we must not allow such a storm of conscience to shatter the peace his Word creates.

God's Word whispers peace when self-doubt storms. Paul says, if you are "in Christ Jesus" (v. 1), "you are controlled not by the sinful nature but by the Spirit" (v. 9). Scripture calms the storm of self-doubt by assuring believers they do have power over the sins they fear will overwhelm them. Consider these words in their full context:

> [8]Those controlled by the sinful nature cannot please God.
> [9]You, however, are controlled not by the sinful nature but by the Spirit, if the Spirit of God lives in you. And if anyone does not have the Spirit of Christ, he does not belong to Christ. [10]But if Christ is in you, your body is dead because of sin, yet your spirit is alive because of righteousness. [11]And if the Spirit of him who raised Jesus from the dead is living in you, he who raised Christ from the

dead will also give life to your mortal bodies through his Spirit, who lives in you.

If you are in Christ Jesus, you are controlled by the Spirit who also gives "life to your mortal bodies." What does that mean? It means you are not merely freed from the guilt of sin by the sacrifice of Christ, you are freed from the power of sin by the Spirit of God at work in you. Your bodies are not lifeless puppets controlled by passions beyond you. God puts the life of his Spirit in you and gives you power over the destructive forces of sin just as he gave Jesus power over the grave.

Satan's Lie

Paul will not let us just spiritualize away what this means. He says your mortal bodies, once slaves to sin and therefore dead in it (Rom. 7:9, 14), are now alive (Rom. 8:11). The implications follow: You have a new obligation to *live* in accord with your new nature (v. 12); and, though you were once dead in sin, by the Spirit you *can* now fulfill this obligation by putting to death the misdeeds of the body (v. 13). You are not weak if the Spirit of God lives in you.

Satan would love for Christians to believe otherwise. Sometimes we want to believe otherwise so that we have an excuse to sin. We plaintively cry, "I can't help it. It's just the way I am. I am so weak. I am so awful. Why should God expect me to be different? I don't even expect me to be different. I just can't help it." This is a lie, a lie Satan uses to defeat us, and a lie we use to excuse sin. The Bible says, "Greater is he that is in you than he that is in the world" (1 John 4:4). We are controlled not by the sinful nature but by the Spirit of God. In the words of classic theology, once we were *not* able *not* to sin, but now we *are* able not to sin. Once the Spirit of God entered our hearts, power over sin entered our lives (Rom. 8:8–9). God says so, and that must still the storm of self-doubt that keeps us despairing and keeps us sinning.

Goose Truth

In late autumn my family likes to travel to southern Illinois around Horseshoe Lake where the geese are flying. Each time we go I am reminded of how foolish it is to believe that God would make Christians helpless to resist the destructive forces of sin.

Highway 3 is the main traffic artery through southern Illinois, and it slices right across the southern flyway of thousands of migrating waterfowl. When you travel far enough south down Highway 3, you see the grain fields the conservation people have planted for the geese. The birds gather in this reserve by the hundreds of thousands. From a distance as you approach the reserve, it looks as though someone has shaken pepper over acres and acres of ground. Then as you get closer you begin to realize the pepper grains are moving and each grain is a goose. The birds blanket the ground until sunset.

Then at dusk an amazing change occurs. Like huge puffs of smoke the birds rise from the ground by the thousands and cross the highway. Why? You would think it would be far easier to fly during the day.

The old-timers of the region conjecture the reason. One side of the highway is a game reserve. The other side of the road is private farmland where hunters gather by the score. The old-timers say the reason the birds wait till sunset to cross that road is that they have learned the hunters' time limit is over at sundown. Wow, if a goose with a pea brain, driven by instinct, has the ability to change behaviors that would lead to its own destruction, how can we with the mind of Christ and controlled by the Spirit of God claim that we cannot change destructive behaviors?

Our weakness is a lie we learn at Satan's knee to tell ourselves. Although no one is going to reach perfection in this life, it is not true that believers are incapable of change. The Spirit of God gives us the truth that we can use his strength, and he provides it when we seek his help in prayer, in biblical instruction, and from Christian counsel. We must not buy the lie that says life cannot be different. God has already made us different. We Christians are no longer under the control of sin if we remember that the Spirit of God has made us stronger than any temptation.

The Bible says, "I can do all things through Christ who strengthens me" (Phil. 4:13). Therefore, I must not believe the lie that says I cannot walk away, resist the sin, or keep control. I must not submit to the despair that says I am powerless against my own passions. Above all I must remember that no matter how weak I feel, God assures me in his Word that I am stronger than the sin that confronts me. I can change. Because God's Spirit is in me, God's strength is in me. I can resist. If necessary I must, without pride in self, seek God's counselors who will assist me in my resistance of sin. But I can rest assured that God has not left me to be tormented by temptations greater than the aid he provides (1 Cor. 10:13). I am not helpless. I am not hopeless. I am not dead in sin. God by his Spirit has given me power over my greatest spiritual enemies. This Spirit of God now grants me peace amidst the storms of self-doubt by granting me strength against the forces of Satan. No longer Satan's puppet, I am controlled by the Spirit who grants life and peace (Rom. 8:6).

Calming the Storm of Self-Rejection

The storms of self-blame and self-doubt whimper away when confronted with the Word of God. But there is yet an angry squall of conscience that sinners must navigate, one that contains the most devastating winds anyone can face. In Romans 8 Paul says that God provides peace of conscience against the storms of self-blame and self-doubt *if* the Spirit of God lives in you (v. 9), *if* Christ is in you (v. 10), and *if* the Spirit of him who raised Jesus from the dead is living in you (v. 11). Any questions? Sure. What if Christ and his Spirit are not in you? My friend Jim cried, "I am not good, I am not strong," and he concluded, "I cannot be God's." Perhaps you too know this cry. It is the ultimate despair that blows from the storm of self-rejection. You find it impossible to believe you could be guilty of such serious sin as may characterize your past or present and still be God's.

Spiritual Evidence

To some extent you must listen carefully to the cries of conscience that blow from this storm. It is true that a life in rebellion against God, a heart that is hardened, or a lifestyle of sin may truly be indications that a person is not God's. You cannot calm a storm of conscience where there is no conscience. But interestingly that is just the point. If you have a spiritually sensitive conscience, then despite the presence of sin you can still claim the gospel of peace, because such a conscience is itself evidence of the Spirit of God in you. The evidence that you are God's is not an absence of sin but your conscience stricken by sin. You can know this from God's Word.

Why do Christians ever doubt they are the Lord's? Because of their guilt for the sin that they know grieves God and is against his plan and purposes. They believe God will no longer accept them because of what they have done against him. But every Christian should consider this vital question when he or she decides whether such a conclusion is warranted: From where comes this guilt for sin and grief for the loss of relationship with God? It is certain that Satan does not want Christians to sorrow for sin or be concerned about a loss of relationship with God. If Satan does not put conviction for sin in their hearts, then who does? The answer, of course, is the Spirit of God who alone puts true sorrow for sin in Christians' hearts. Grief over sin is inherent evidence of the Spirit in Christians and, therefore, of God's continuing claim upon them. God's Word proves what their hearts may doubt, which is that apart from God there is no true sorrow for sin:

> ⁶The mind of sinful man is death, but the mind controlled by the Spirit is life and peace, ⁷because the sinful mind is hostile to God. It does not submit to God's law, nor can it do so.

The mind that is not controlled by the Spirit of God does not truly sorrow for sin. It cannot do so. Such a mind is hostile to God. It does not care that God has been hurt, or his purposes damaged, because such a mind cannot truly fathom the awfulness of sin. When Christians' hearts grieve in sorrow over sin, they are witnessing the presence of the Spirit in them, because apart from the Spirit there could be no such grief.

Earthly Horror

I have never seen a more vivid example of a spiritual void in a heart incapable of sorrowing over sin than once during another trip with my brother Gordon, just as he was preparing to enter the Air Force. Because Gordon was getting ready to enter the military, he sympathized with anyone already in uniform. When we passed a hitchhiker in army fatigues along a lonely section of highway in Kentucky, Gordon insisted we stop. He said he wanted to be helpful, but what he really wanted was a pep talk from somebody already in the military to assure him he had made a good decision in enlisting. The fellow we picked up did not fit the bill.

The young hitchhiker was on his way out of the military and did not mind telling us why. He told us military life was terrible. He said in the armed forces everybody takes advantage of you, and no one supports you when trouble comes. His words were so bitter and his manner so agitated that Gordon began to wonder if he had just made the worst decision of his life. He had to know. So he mustered the courage to ask our rider if he was upset about military life in general, or if something specific had made him so angry. That was when the real story poured out.

The soldier told us he had been a squad leader with a group of American soldiers under the direction of a Lt. William Calley when they had gone into a small village in Vietnam named My Lai. There, as the rest of the world now knows, these young Americans—raised in towns and homes no different from our own—lined up and savagely slaughtered old men, women, and children in this village suspected of having Viet Cong sympathizers. The squad leader told us his story: what he had done, why he thought he was justified, and how the army responded when word got to the press.

We drove on and let our passenger off at his destination. When he was out of the car, my brother and I faced one another feeling much older than we had been only minutes before. The horror of a war a world away had suddenly come closer than we had ever experienced. We were not shaken merely because of whom we had picked up but because of his perspective. My brother said, "He doesn't even think what he did was wrong. He can't even see it. There is not one ounce of remorse in him. He's not sorry for what he did, only for what he thinks the army did to him."

Words of Scripture our father had often quoted to us as children as he tried to help us understand our world came flooding into our minds: "The natural man receiveth not the things of the Spirit of God: for they are foolishness unto him: neither can he know them, because they are spiritually discerned" (1 Cor. 2:14 KJV). My brother and I know now more than ever before that apart from the working of the Spirit, men do not even discern their sin; they see only what has disadvantaged them. True spiritual understanding can be explained only by the presence of the Spirit.

Heavenly Proof

The case of the hitchhiker is extreme, of course, but the truth it underscores is vital for everyday living. Sorrow for sin that makes us doubt we are God's is, in fact, the evidence that we are God's. Were we not his, our sorrow would be selfish, self-centered, and even hostile toward God.

How do you distinguish true spiritual sorrow from selfish human sorrow? Paul tells you very clearly. He says, "Those who are led by the Spirit of God are sons of God. For you did not receive a Spirit . . . to fear, but . . . of Sonship. And by him we cry 'Abba, Father'" (Rom. 8:14–15). To know whether you are a child of God, do not ask whether your life is sinless, but whether your heart is Son-like. Do you still long for his love? Do you grieve for his hurt? Do you ache for the pain of him who gave his only Son for you? When your spirit cries out in love for your heavenly Father, then it testifies of the Spirit of God in you that marks you as a child of God. Such love leads you to the Father in new confession, new obedience, and new assurance of your relationship with him, despite past failure. When the heart cries out, "Abba, Daddy," the heavenly Father experiences joy and the child's heart knows peace.

Do you sense, as Paul did, your obligation to the Father who loves you because of his grace (v. 12)? The clearest answer may be found in an honest response to the question, When you sorrow for sin, for whom are you sorry? I do not claim the real answer always lies on the surface of your thoughts. Sometimes you must search deep into your heart to find the truth. But if the truth you find is this, Yes, I sorrow for my God, my Father, then you have mined the gold that is eternal security. For even in the midst of a storm of conscience over sin, you may have this peace: The Spirit testifies with my spirit that I am a child of God because by the Spirit only can I cry out, "Oh, Daddy, I am sorry." My heart aches for him; my spirit yearns for him. This can only be by the Spirit of God. By this Spirit I have the peace of knowing I am God's own.

Francis Scott Key, author of "The Star-Spangled Banner," caught the essence of these truths in his hymn, "Lord, with Glowing Heart I'd Praise Thee." Wrote Key: "Praise the grace whose threats alarmed thee; praise the grace that whispers peace." The grace that convicts my heart of sin and causes me to fear the wrath of God is the same grace that whispers peace, because I could not fear without grace already at work in me. Thus, even when I hate my sin, I do not fear God's hate. My antipathy for my sin is my assurance of God's love. The storm of self-rejection cannot destroy my peace because its blasts prove I am anchored in God's acceptance.

God's Peace

When I was a child, I had a friend who had a great deal of trouble learning to read. The school pushed him, his parents pushed him, even his friends pushed him. Those were the days before much was known about learning disabilities or their diagnosis. Our school, not fully understanding the problem, told his parents the reason this child was not succeeding was that he was not trying. His parents responded by punishing him for not reading well enough or fast enough. The result was the boy became so stressed that he developed a nervous habit of squinting his eyes each time he blinked. Whenever the stress got too great, and this sometimes went on for months, he would squint/blink. I look back on that time and ache for all such children. I resolved never to put my own through such things.

My resolve was not strong enough. Only a few weeks after my older son Colin started kindergarten, he brought his first school friend home for the day. They arrived at lunchtime, and my son was practically bouncing off the walls with excitement. His first request was to take his friend upstairs to see his room. Unfortunately, his room was right beside our baby's room, and the baby had just gone to sleep.

I could sense how important it was for Colin to show off his special things, so I said he could take his friend upstairs *if they were quiet.* The two little boys had been upstairs no more than two minutes when they started playing trampoline on the beds and shrieking in glee. I marched up the stairs to remind them they were supposed to be quiet, the baby was asleep, and there had better be no more loud noise.

I did not realize how excited Colin was. I was less than halfway back down the stairs when I heard the loud bop of a plastic bat on a kindergartner's head followed by my son shouting at the top of his lungs, "I gotcha!" That did it. I marched right back into the room and in front of his friend I got after Colin.

I told him I did not care how special the day was or whom he had with him; he still had to obey me. There was going to be no more playing in his room. I said I had trusted him, but he had not honored my trust. I ordered him downstairs and said there had better be no more noise.

Not all my words were wrong, but they came too shrilly, too loudly, with too much vehemence and too little understanding. Picture the scene. The excitement of this afternoon has been building for days, the baby in the next room is now screaming, the new school friend is watching (in gaping, open-mouthed terror), an angry father is hovering over his son, Colin is fighting for all he is worth to keep the welling tears from overflowing, and I end by saying, "Do you understand me, young man?" He replied, "Yes, sir," and his eyes squinted/blinked at me.

Arghh! That stressed blink cut me in two. What had I done? I hated even to consider what that stress signal said about me as a parent. How could I have been so dumb? How could I have been so weak? How could I be so awful to my own son? A thousand self-denunciations knifed my heart. Is this all I've learned? Is this all the work God has done in me? Is he really in me? If he is in me, how could I do this with all I'm supposed to know and all I'm supposed to be?

At that moment I not only hated the sin, I wasn't very fond of myself either. My wife, Kathy, asked me later that afternoon what was wrong, because I was acting so strangely. I hated telling her. Something in me had shattered a bit—my own image of the parent I thought I was and the person I wanted to be.

I cannot tell you that my own disappointment in myself miraculously disappeared after that day or that I found some magic glue to restore my self-image. I believe it is healthier that I did not, because as a result, I was forced to find my inner peace in something more solid than my own character. The peace I found was not in my perfection as a parent but in the truths of Romans 8:1–16.

I will claim that peace because, though I was wrong, my Savior says there is no condemnation. Though I was weak, I am not destined to repeat other parents' errors— I have the Spirit who strengthens and enables me to change. And though I did not reflect my heavenly Father well that day, I still long to call him *Abba,* which means he still delights to call me son.

Praise the grace that reveals the spiritual dangers that should alarm us. Praise that same grace that amidst the storms of conscience yet whispers, "Peace, be still."

QUESTIONS *for Thought*

1. What does Satan want you to believe about your power to resist sinful urges and patterns?
2. How can Christians be sure there is no temptation over which they have no control?
3. What makes Christians sometimes doubt that God will accept them?
4. How may anxiety about your relationship with God be evidence of spiritual life in you?

PART TWO

Spirit Signs

THREE

Dance of Joy

In an attic somewhere I have a newspaper given to me by my mother. She saved it when World War II ended. In large, six-inch type the paper's headline declares, "PEACE." When the word spread in her Tennessee town that the dying was over, she told me, the people poured out of their homes and businesses to dance in the streets. My mom danced in the streets! Now, that must have been something, because she was raised an old-school Methodist, and they just didn't do that sort of thing. The explanation is easy. When there was life and peace after so much dying, spontaneous joy had to flow. Overflowing, wondrous, beautiful joy always flows when a war is over.

In Romans 8 Paul writes in the context of another war—a spiritual war. Here too is fighting and dying. At the end of chapter 7 Paul speaks of a war that has raged inside of him and he cries out, "Who will rescue me from this body of death?" Paul answers with the name of his Savior, "Jesus Christ our Lord." As a bugle call pierces the noise of battle with a message of hope, the name of the Savior is Paul's victory note. Because of Jesus this internal war too can end. The spiritual forces that threaten our souls with eternal death have been defeated. Though war preoccupies Paul's thought in chapter 7, by the sixth verse of chapter 8 the apostle declares "life and peace."

What must be the result of this war's signaled end? Joy flows. That is why the Westminster Catechism's authors determined that if one of God's sure promises to Christian believers is peace, then joy must follow. Believers are promised not only peace of conscience but joy of a very particular nature. God does not necessarily promise joy in stock market results, nor joy in World Series outcomes, nor joy in personal success of any kind. Using Old English terms, the author said God promises Christians *joy in the Holy Ghost*. What did they mean by that? They borrowed the term from Romans 14:17, but the background explanation is in Romans 8. The Holy Spirit is mentioned at least eighteen times in this chapter—more often than in any other portion of Scripture. This is the great passage on the work of the Spirit. The meaning of joy in the Holy Spirit is to be found in these verses. Here God publishes the news that Satan's war is done and through the Spirit invites all Christians to join in heaven's dance of joy. Listen to the music of the Spirit:

Romans 8:5–28
⁵Those who live according to the sinful nature have their minds set on what that nature desires; but those who live in accordance with the Spirit have their minds set on what

the Spirit desires. [6]The mind of sinful man is death, but the mind controlled by the Spirit is life and peace; [7]the sinful mind is hostile to God. It does not submit to God's law, nor can it do so. [8]Those controlled by the sinful nature cannot please God.

[9]You, however, are controlled not by the sinful nature but by the Spirit, if the Spirit of God lives in you. And if anyone does not have the Spirit of Christ, he does not belong to Christ. [10]But if Christ is in you, your body is dead because of sin, yet your spirit is alive because of righteousness. [11]And if the Spirit of him who raised Jesus from the dead is living in you, he who raised Christ from the dead will also give life to your mortal bodies through his Spirit, who lives in you.

[12]Therefore, brothers, we have an obligation—but it is not to the sinful nature, to live according to it. [13]For if you live according to the sinful nature, you will die; but if by the Spirit you put to death the misdeeds of the body, you will live, [14]because those who are led by the Spirit of God are sons of God. [15]For you did not receive a spirit that makes you a slave again to fear, but you received the Spirit of sonship. And by him we cry, "*Abba*, Father." [16]The Spirit himself testifies with our spirit that we are God's children. [17]Now if we are children, then we are heirs—heirs of God and co-heirs with Christ, if indeed we share in his sufferings in order that we may also share in his glory.

[18]I consider that our present sufferings are not worth comparing with the glory that will be revealed in us. [19]The creation waits in eager expectation for the sons of God to be revealed. [20]For the creation was subjected to frustration, not by its own choice, but by the will of the one who subjected it, in hope [21]that the creation itself will be liberated from its bondage to decay and brought into the glorious freedom of the children of God.

[22]We know that the whole creation has been groaning as in the pains of childbirth right up to the present time. [23]Not only so, but we ourselves, who have the firstfruits of the Spirit, groan inwardly as we wait eagerly for our adoption as sons, the redemption of our bodies. [24]For in

this hope we were saved. But hope that is seen is no hope at all. Who hopes for what he already has? ²⁵But if we hope for what we do not yet have, we wait for it patiently.

²⁶In the same way, the Spirit helps us in our weakness. We do not know what we ought to pray for, but the Spirit himself intercedes for us with groans that words cannot express. ²⁷And he who searches our hearts knows the mind of the Spirit, because the Spirit intercedes for the saints in accordance with God's will.

²⁸And we know that in all things God works for the good of those who love him, who have been called according to his purpose.

Seeing the Spirit

Our friends said they could not wait to tell us the good news. They drove from a town where I had been their pastor and dropped in unexpectedly. They were so excited they could hardly contain themselves. The wife, Betty, was nearly weeping with joy as she told why they had come.

For about three years Betty had been witnessing to a next-door neighbor who was a cult member. The two were on friendly terms and had many good talks as each tried to teach the other the meaning of true faith. We occasionally prayed for these talks at our church's prayer meetings and suggested Scripture for Betty to discuss with her friend.

Then, for some reason Betty could not discern, the relationship took a bad turn. Every discussion ended in heated words and anger. The neighbor began to criticize Betty, her faith, and her church. Time after time Betty came to our meetings hurt and tearful, asking what she should do. We prayed and suggested she simply keep presenting the Word of God as lovingly as possible. Regardless of what her neighbor said, we encouraged Betty to try to maintain the friendship. She was determined to try and decided that if the relationship were to be broken, it would have to be the friend who broke it. Eventually that happened.

The relationship shattered over a rosebush. Betty and her husband planted a rosebush in their yard near the neighbor's property. The neighbor called, outraged that they would plant that "thorn bush" near her fence without asking. She said she would never speak to them again. And she did not, for about six months.

Then one day without any prior notice, Betty answered a gentle knock at her door. It was the neighbor. She told Betty she was leaving the cult. She said she knew what Betty had been saying all those months was right. She could see the truth in Scripture. She said she just hated to face her mistakes and had done everything she could, even getting mad about the location of the rosebush, to keep from facing them. Now, she said, she wanted to become a Christian.

When Betty told us the news, she could not restrain her joy. Tears streamed down her face as she spoke. Her voice trembled with a bubbling laughter that seemed to punctuate almost every sentence. The room virtually glowed with her smile. But the joy was not simply for what her neighbor had learned. Betty had discovered something too. She concluded her news by saying, "I've never had any trouble seeing the Father or seeing the Son, but this is the first time I think I've really seen the Spirit, and it is so great!"

Betty had seen the working of the Spirit in the changing of a heart and the saving of a soul. By seeing this work, she now knew the Spirit in such a way that her joy overflowed. It is a joy all Christians can share, because in Romans 8:5–28 Paul shows the working of the Spirit. Here believers may see what the Holy Spirit performs *in them, for them,* and *through them.* If they are able to see the work of the Holy Spirit as Paul describes it, then they will be able to share in the joy an apostle expressed centuries ago and a dear saint named Betty experienced today.

Creation of New Life

Paul begins to share his joy by telling of *the work of the Spirit in us.* The apostle describes the *creation of a new life* in all Christians (vv. 9–11). He concludes in verse 11:

> And if the Spirit of him who raised Jesus from the dead is living in you, he who raised Christ from the dead will also give life to your mortal bodies through his Spirit, who lives in you.

As God breathed the spirit of life into man at the creation, God now breathes the Holy Spirit into Christians so that their bodies and spirits are alive in a new way (see John 20:22). What was characterized by death, decay, and the domination of sin is now characterized by eternal life, spiritual healing, and power over sin. Christians are new creations, fundamentally different than they were before the Spirit entered their hearts. Now the same power that raised Jesus from the dead resides in them. They have new life where only death was possible previously. This new life is cause for great joy.

Vital Signs

We need only look to our own experiences to know what joy there is when life comes where only death was expected. In a hospital near us a newborn baby stretches and yawns as though his life is no more challenging than a summer afternoon in the shade. We know differently. The newspapers call this child Baby John. While Baby John was still in his mother's womb, physicians discerned that his heart was defective. He would soon die. So before he was even born, the doctors determined he should have a heart transplant. At just the right time, doctors delivered Baby John from the womb where death awaited him and gave him a new heart. Where once there could only be death there is life. We are amazed. His parents are overjoyed.

Christians should be able to identify with Baby John's parents in their joy, because it so reflects their spiritual experience. Before they were ever born God discerned their hearts to be defective. They were hopelessly damaged by their sin nature, the inherited trait all humans share (see Rom. 5:12–18). All were doomed to spiritual death by those hearts. But God delivers them. He takes hearts that were as spiritually lifeless as stone—cold and hostile to God—and transforms them into hearts that are warm and tender toward him (see Ezek. 36:26). God breathes his Holy Spirit into Christians and they live. Their hearts beat with a spiritual life that would be impossible without the Spirit transplanting his life into them. They have new natures, new abilities, and new desires because of the hearts the Spirit creates in them. In fact, these new features of their being are vital signs that their new hearts are functioning.

Discussion in the previous chapter underscored the fact that our hearts' longing for the Father (the love for *Abba* replacing natural hostility toward God) is a proof we are the Lord's. But this attitude change is simply the culminating evidence of new life. There is much more in this passage to help us confirm that our new hearts are functioning as they should. Think of Baby John in the hospital. Wires and tubes of various kinds seem to dangle from almost every square inch of his little body. Monitors and life-support systems line the walls of his room. The doctors are chiefly concerned for his heart, but they monitor scores of other vital signs to make sure the transplanted organ is operating properly. The apostle Paul records the vital signs of a Spirit-transplanted heart in this passage so that we can monitor the health of our hearts and know the joy of seeing vital signs of new life in us.

The vital signs of a heart made new by the Spirit readily distinguish it from the old. Paul says an individual supplied with life by the old heart is controlled by its defective nature: "The sinful mind is hostile to God. It does not submit to God's law, nor can it do so. Those controlled by the sinful nature cannot please God" (Rom. 8:7–8). In contrast to a life with a defective heart, a life with the new heart supplied by the Spirit has these vital signs:

New desires (v. 5)
New abilities (v. 9)
New sense of obligation (v. 12)
New deeds (vv. 13–14)

New hearts result in new and different lives. Progress may not be rapid in all areas or constant in all periods; nonetheless, fundamental changes are inevitable when a new heart begins to beat in a person.

Consider the difference in Baby John since he has a new heart. His entire being shows the effects of the life now in him. Where there was lethargy and caring for nothing, there are new desires (if only for food at this point). Fingers are beginning to move. Soon he will be able to raise arms and legs. He does what he could not do before he received his new heart. Once there was not even enough life in him to long for a parent. Now he cries for the touch of his mother. New desires, new deeds, new affections are all vital signs of a new heart functioning well both physically and spiritually.

Profound Joy

Of course, not all of Baby John's problems in life are over now. He is not very strong yet. His personality is still in the making. In the future he is sure to face the battery of childhood illnesses, the insecurities of adolescence, and the challenges of adulthood. But he has new life in his body. He has a new heart in evidence. All future problems dissolve into insignificance in the face of this one overwhelming fact. Baby John is alive! He is a living, breathing child. Because his heart has now been made right, he is not just a corpse waiting to happen. He is a son. The profound joy provided by a child's life creates a joy we should sense and share, because, the apostle says, we Christians have received "the Spirit of sonship" (v. 15). We are saved from death and can live as children of God eternally because the Spirit has given us new hearts. What joy should now be ours, even in the face of life's difficulties, because of the amazing work the Holy Spirit has already done in our hearts.

We may still be weak. We have not fully attained the spiritual maturity God intends for us. There may still be troubles ahead. But regardless of the difficulties around us or in us, the Holy Spirit has given us life. Our aliveness is a fact so profound and so beautiful in its eternal significance that it cannot be eclipsed by temporal difficulties or disappointments.

Suppose Baby John's doctors had come to his parents after the operation and said, "Baby John's new heart is doing fine, but we have some bad news. He is very fair skinned and in his teen years may develop acne." Do you think the parents would have wept? Of course not. They would have said, "He's alive! Who cares if he has skin problems later?" News about the baby's heart makes concern about whether he will have skin blemishes when he is sixteen incidental.

Even if the doctors had reported something more serious, such as a twisted leg that would need additional operations, the parents' joy would have been tempered but not destroyed. Why? Because Baby John lives. The news of life itself is so overwhelming that it pushes all other concerns to secondary status and perpetuates joy even in the face of great trauma. The news of spiritual life should affect Christians the same way.

When the vital signs of the Spirit indicate we have been set free from the power of sin and death forever, we should be overwhelmed with joy. Our gladness may at times be tempered by present or anticipated difficulties, but where there is life there is joy. Much in our culture that passes for faith, which attaches Christian joy to the acquisition of material or physical blessing, misinterprets how marvelous is the work of the Spirit in granting us life. The religion that preaches Christians do not have sufficient cause for joy until they are prospering in this world has not perceived the magnitude of the Spirit's blessing, which reaches beyond this world.

Only the most carnal of religions promises to reward selfishness. Christianity promises to allow believers to sacrifice everything for the sake of their faith because their most precious possession—life itself—is eternally secured by the Holy Spirit. Far from tying joy to the blessings of this world, true faith and the great defenders of it have always tried to unshackle joy from this life's mirages of happiness and tied it to the miracle of the Spirit's dwelling in the Christian.

When John Wesley came to Georgia to evangelize Indians, he stepped from shipboard into the path of a Moravian Brethren elder. Said Wesley, "How do I minister here?" The elder responded, "First I must ask you, are you a Christian?" Wesley replied, "I think that I am." The insightful elder quoted Romans 8, saying, "I did not ask what you think. Are you a Christian? Does the Spirit of God testify with your spirit that you are a child of God?" Eventually Wesley told the elder that yes, of course, he was a child of God. But Wesley later wrote in his diary, "Those were vain words."

Why did Wesley feel his profession of faith was vain? He recorded the reason. In his diary Wesley wrote how he had witnessed other Moravian Christians joyfully singing hymns on the voyage from England despite life-threatening storms that had sent him cowering and despairing. Those Christians had a joy that even the threat of death could not shatter. Wesley knew his joy was far more fragile and far less secure. He later wrote that prior to his conversion at Aldersgate, where he "felt his heart strangely warmed," what led him to doubt his former claims of faith was that he did not know and could not share the pervading joy of Peter Boehler, another Moravian friend, who let no adversity quench his joyful spirit. The Spirit of God did not testify with Wesley's spirit that he was a child of God, because he was missing the vital sign of joy in the aliveness the Spirit provides.

What Wesley recognized as a central distinctive of true faith is the joy promised to all believers, joy that is greater than all their sin and adversity. It is the joy resulting from the truth that where there was death, now there is life through the Spirit which can be detected through his work in believers' hearts.

So fundamental is the joy that accompanies the knowledge of new life, that Christians must develop a healthy caution of those teachers for whom this truth is not enough. Those who think they need extra signs, extra wealth, and easy circumstances to have sufficient cause for real joy do not understand the true source of believers' joy. In a similar vein Christians must be careful to choose leaders who not only mouth the truths of God's grace but have the joy that reflects an intimate knowledge of his Spirit. Regardless of what difficulties they face, all Christians must be ever diligent to remember the greatness of the truth that they already have the greatest gift of all—life in the Spirit. If they forget this deep well of ever-dependable joy, they are doomed to measure their joy by the shifting sands of their circumstances, their achievements, or their acceptance. They must remember they have access to an infinite reservoir of happiness in the life the Spirit provides and have the privilege of tasting its refreshment even when their world turns to desert.

God provides his Holy Spirit because he desires our testimony and delights in our joy. Of course, there are many reasons for solemnity and seriousness, but these matters do not require us to dispense with the foundational joy that pleases him as well as us. We Christians can and should strive for joy. God sent his Holy Spirit for us to receive and to reflect the wonders of new life in him. This new life is not without difficulty and even tragedy, but neither is it without the deep assurance of God's eternal love. The grace the Holy Spirit reveals shines brightly enough to radiate joy even through the dark clouds that come into every life.

Christian leaders especially should remember the importance of a testimony of joy. Many things can frustrate and anger Christian leaders in the fight for the gospel: deadness, intransigence, license. As a result, too many sheep are served by shepherds lost in the crises of the moment, distracted from the wonder of new life in Christ Jesus. Such shepherds feed their flocks on the gospels of suspicion of others, defense of self, and pride of orthodoxy. They preach without peace, minister without selflessness, and live without joy. God's leaders must not lose the joy of the Spirit of life in themselves, regardless of what they face, or they offer nothing but heartache to sheep who need new hearts.

Confirmation of New Position

As wonderful as is the creation of new life in us, it is but the beginning of the work of the Holy Spirit that God reveals in Romans 8. Along with descriptions of the Spirit's work **in** us, Paul highlights *the work of the Spirit for us.* He makes it clear that we Christians also have wonderful cause for joy in the way that the Spirit *confirms our new position* as heirs of God.

The Court of Heaven

Paul paints a courtroom scene with the words of this passage (see vv. 16–17). A probate court is in session. A vast estate must be claimed. The estate is the kingdom of God. Only the heirs will share in its glorious riches. Any questions? Sure. Who are the heirs? Or more specifically, Am I an heir? If I am, how can I know? How can I prove it?

Paul answers with the standard of a Jewish court, letting every matter be established by at least two witnesses. Our own spirits testify that we are children of God with the evidence that we love him as *Abba,* Father. But for each of us this is only one witness. Therefore the apostle says, "The Spirit Himself testifies with our spirit that we are God's children." By testifying for us the Spirit confirms our new position as heirs of the kingdom before the court of heaven. Paul concludes, "Now if we are children, then we are heirs— heirs of God and co-heirs with Christ." The vital signs that confirmed new life in us are now pieces of evidence presented by the Spirit for us to corroborate our lineage. His testimony is unimpeachable, and therefore our inheritance is secure. We shall receive the glories of the kingdom as God's own children since we are co-heirs with Christ.

Now, if we are heirs of God's kingdom, what can rob us of joy? Paul says in verse 18, "I consider that our present sufferings are not worth comparing with the glory that will be revealed in us." In contrast to those who claim that Christianity puts you on easy street, Paul says heirs of the kingdom suffer. In fact, he says we must suffer if our character reflects true kinship with the Son of God, who was persecuted and afflicted in this fallen world (see v. 17). But even suffering does not deprive believers of joy, because these afflictions are light and momentary compared with the exceeding weight of eternal glory that is assuredly ours because of the testimony of the Spirit (see 2 Cor. 4:17). Joy continues in the face of difficulty because we know the afflictions that bring us genuine pain will culminate in the kingdom that brings us glorious reward.

The Confidence of an Heir

When I was in seminary, I met the heir to a local chemical company fortune. However, I did not know the person I had met was an heir until he walked away from me. I had been invited by some church friends to a fancy dinner party. I was feeling terribly out of place among all the finery and high-society manners, when a fellow about my age drifted over to talk. He seemed even more out of place than I was. Amid the tuxedos and black ties he wore tattered blue jeans, an old plaid shirt, and a pair of wafflestomper boots. He seemed totally oblivious to his apparent poverty and inappropriate attire. In fact, he exuded a carefree confidence. Only when he walked away and I was told who he was did I understand why. He was wealthy beyond my imagining.

Because his father wanted him to experience "real life," the chemical-fortune heir was currently living without the full benefits of his wealth. But he was not distraught because of his rags or because he did not fit in at a dinner party. The riches that were assuredly his as an heir made these things meaningless concerns. His inheritance made him confident even in the face of present difficulties. In fact, lack of concern about his present poverty was this heir's virtual flaunting of his future wealth.

We are heirs of glory. The Holy Spirit confirms our inheritance in our hearts and before God. This does not mean that all things are suddenly easy or that we have all the benefits of the kingdom right now. We may need to live a testimony of joy amid real hardships so that others can witness the reality of grace in us. For now, Paul says, we live in a fallen world, a world so troubled that all of creation groans as in the pains of childbirth waiting for Christ's return when the inheritance is distributed and when all is made right again (Rom. 8:19–22). Christians are not unaffected by this fallen condition. We too have cause to groan as we wait for the redemption of our bodies. Until that day these bodies, like the fallen world in which we live, are subject to suffering and decay (v. 23). But in the light of the testimony of the Holy Spirit, we can be confident of our inheritance and constant in joy despite present difficulties.

The Inheritance of a Son

Even the frailties of our bodies do not deprive us of the deeper joy of knowing the decay will end, glory will come, and we shall reap an inheritance, the rewards of which will make the trials of this life distant memories of momentary pain. The Bible says our entire lives are but a "handbreadth" in God's eternal time frame. Even if there is intense pain now, it is like the passing pain of childbirth, which is immediately dulled by the presence of new life that is the culmination and reward for the suffering. New life in glory is sufficient cause for present joy even in the face of terrible affliction.

A Christian friend has a son named Justin who suffers from Tourette's syndrome, a genetic disorder that causes its victims to experience uncontrolled body twitches and utter odd noises. Though medication can sometimes help control the spasms, there is no cure. One day when my friend was traveling away from home, his wife took Justin and his two sisters to a burger restaurant as a relief from Dad's absence. The relief was not to come. Just as the hamburgers were unwrapped, the syndrome began to affect

Justin again. As his noises and jerks grew more obvious, the mother decided it was best to leave and eat at home.

Going home early from an outing because of Justin was no new experience for this family, but for some reason it was harder on one of his sisters this time. As she left the restaurant, she looked at her mother with tears brimming in her eyes and asked, "Mommy, is Justin always going to be this way?"

Later when the young mother related the hurting daughter's question to her husband, her own eyes filled with tears. "What did you answer?" he asked. She turned her face to the wall to hide the tears that now came in a rush and said, "I didn't have any answer."

"Oh yes, you did," said the husband as he held her. "You can say Justin will not always be this way. There will come a time when Justin will get his inheritance from God. He will not hurt anymore. We won't cry anymore. Justin loves the Lord Jesus, and God says he will redeem his children's bodies as well as their souls. Justin will not always be this way."

Christian joy is not "pie in the sky by and by." Our joy begins now, because we realize that the workings of the Spirit we witness today are only the "firstfruits" (v. 23) of the bounty that is to come. The afflictions of the world may still strike, but by the Spirit we can face them assured that they will end and we will have our full inheritance of redeemed bodies and souls. That is why other Scriptures refer to the Holy Spirit as our "surety." The Spirit is the guarantor that the house made without hands and reserved in heaven for us, cannot be denied to the heirs of the kingdom (see 2 Cor. 5:1). In that heavenly home there will be "no more death or mourning or crying or pain" (Rev. 21:4). We shall reside there because the Holy Spirit confirms it as our inheritance. This confirmation is a constant source of joy our lives often require and our world cannot restrain.

QUESTIONS
for Thought

1. If we cannot actually see the Holy Spirit, how do we know that he is present?
2. What are the vital signs of new life in a Christian?
3. How does the Spirit of God bear witness with your spirit that you are a child of God?
4. How does the testimony of God's Spirit grant us confidence to face the trials of the present and the future?

FOUR

Power in Prayer

Channel of New Power

The blessings of the Holy Spirit influence not only the world inside of us and the world beyond us. The world around us, also, is affected by the Holy Spirit in marvelous ways. The Spirit works in us—creating new life—and for us—confirming our new position—but the most concrete of blessings for believers results from the work of *the Spirit through us*—making each of us a *channel of new power.*

Three of the most amazing verses in all of Scripture are in this passage from Romans 8:

²⁶In the same way, the Spirit helps us in our weakness. We do not know what we ought to pray, but the Spirit himself intercedes for us with groans that words cannot express. ²⁷And he who searches our hearts knows the mind of the Spirit, because the Spirit intercedes for the saints in accordance with God's will.

²⁸And we know that in all things God works for the good of those who love him, who have been called according to his purpose.

The last verse is one of the most familiar in the Bible. It promises that God will work all things for the good of the believer. What we sometimes forget is that this verse is attached to two preceding verses on prayer. Because of the work of the Holy Spirit, the prayers of believers mold the world into conformity with God's will. We are channels of incalculable power.

The Power of the Spirit in Prayer

Since I was a child I have enjoyed walking the levee along the Mississippi River near my hometown. My favorite spot is just beyond the power plant. There the river has been diverted into a narrow sluice to turn the huge turbines that create the city's power. The water boils down the channel, frothing and tumbling, developing huge waves and deep sinkholes. Large trees and fifty-gallon oil drums are sucked beneath the surface and swirled in gargantuan whirlpools as though they were but toothpicks and thimbles. The noise is the roar of a hundred jet engines.

Still, despite these immediate displays of raw power, I only begin to fathom the immense potential of the river when I look beyond the torrent at dusk to the town's distant lights and realize the entire city thrives because of the flow of water in these few hundred yards of channel.

Then I remember the Spirit who moved upon the face of the waters at creation (Gen. 1:2). The immense power in this small sluice is but a drop in the bucket compared with the power displayed by the Holy Spirit when the world was formed. And it is that same Spirit, the creative instrument of the Godhead, who now lives in me (Rom. 8:9) and energizes my prayers (v. 26). The Holy Spirit is yet creating a world in accord with God's will through my prayers. No force in this world can compare with the power of the Spirit channeled through Christians when they pray.

The Design of the Spirit in Prayer

Unlike the power of the river, the activity of the Holy Spirit is not a swirling turbulence. The Spirit's power is target directed and laser precise. Christians are always taught that God answers their prayers when they pray in accord with his will. But they struggle with this instruction because they find it so difficult to discern his will in specific matters. The Holy Spirit rescues them from their consternation, because the apostle affirms that, even though Christians do not know what to pray (in their human finiteness), the Spirit intercedes for them in accordance with God's will (vv. 26–27).

We should not pretend that we have the mind of God when we pray. Our thoughts will always be limited by human time, human wisdom, and personal perspective. God acts sovereignly with the perspective of a future we cannot discern and perfectly planned consequences we cannot anticipate. That God's thoughts are far above our own, however, is no reason to abandon prayer. The Spirit helps us with the content of our prayers. Even with finite human minds we are enabled to pray in accord with the will of God, because the Spirit takes humble, obedient prayer to God and conforms it to God's will. We offer our desires to God, with our deepest desire being that he would glorify his name and accomplish his purposes, which is just exactly what God does.

We should never be so arrogant as to sidle up to God's throne of grace in our prayers and say, "God, I've got it all figured out. Here's what you're supposed to do." When Jesus taught us to pray to God, he said we should pray "Thy will be done," not "my will be done." Because God has the heart of a heavenly father, this is no risk. We need not fear the will of him who loves us enough to sacrifice his own Son on our behalf. When we humbly confess the limitations of our vision while obediently offering the desires of our hearts, the Holy Spirit molds our prayers into petitions that please God and satisfy our deepest needs.

The Fervor of the Spirit in Prayer

Along with controlling the content of Christians' prayers, the Spirit helps with the fervency of their prayers. The Bible says the Spirit intercedes for believers with groans that words cannot express (v. 26). Some persons understand these words to mean speaking in tongues, but such a meaning seems unlikely. This is the third reference to such "groaning" in this passage. Earlier Paul wrote of creation groaning for the fulfillment of God's purpose. He described those groans as the painful cries of one giving birth (v. 22). In the next verse the apostle says Christians groan with the same pain awaiting the fulfillment of God's purpose for their bodies. Again the reference is to the utterances of great agony. Paul writes that not only does creation groan, not only do Christians groan, but the Spirit groans, interceding for the fulfillment of the Lord's purposes in their lives. With more fervor than they themselves could gather, the Spirit is before the throne of grace crying out, "Holy God, bless them. God of creation, bless them. Heavenly Father, bless them." The Spirit cries as in the agonies of one bearing new life, because new life is being formed. The Father responds to the cries of the Spirit so dear and near to him to make our lives what he wants them to be.

It is a startling realization that the Holy Spirit controls how I pray as well as what I pray. For I recognize at times when I pray for matters of the church, or for other people, or even for my own family, I pray without the urgency I should feel. I may even fall asleep in praying for the souls of those I love. I am too weak to pray as I ought. But still I do not despair in my prayers. The Holy Spirit pleads for me with groans deeper than I can express that touch the heart of the Father. The Spirit of God molds both the content and fervor of my prayers, so I am confident that God's loving, good, and perfect will shall be done. Because of this work of the Spirit "we know that in all things God works for the good of those who love him, who have been called according to his purpose" (v. 28).

The Wonder of the Spirit in Prayer

Here is an amazing discovery: The God of all creation works through my prayers to do his will. I do not have to know all the answers or emote just the right way to be used greatly by him. What a joy to understand the marvelous work of the Spirit in my prayers, not just because of the power for good that may be channeled through me, but because of the burden taken off me. I do not have to say everything right, or do everything right, to have things turn out right.

Through the Spirit, God may even use my mistakes to work good as I seek him in prayer. This does not mean I should carelessly pursue wrong or imprudent actions. My own heart is healthiest when I do everything for God's honor and glory. Yet there are times when I know I have blown it. I have failed to accomplish some goal, or I have said or done something wrong, and in shame and guilt I say to God, "Oh, God, I am so sorry; I let you down." Then I remember the assurances of these verses and God's certain reply: "Do not despair, child, you were not holding me up. I am the sovereign God who works **all** things for good." God does not promise that all seems good in this fallen world, or that all is done with good motives by sinful people, but he does promise that he is sufficient to work all things into his good purposes.

By his Spirit, God channels his power through us so that all things work together for good in response to faithful prayer. No child of God of whatever age or infirmity or limitation is insignificant if this is true. Because of the channeled power of the Spirit there is no more potent force in all creation than an invalid saint in a nursing home praying. In all secular culture there is no more powerful an influence affecting families than a parent kneeling at a child's bedside. In all the church there is no greater ministry than that of a pastor in a small work in an obscure town who petitions God for the work of the kingdom. In each case, regardless of human appearances, there is a force more powerful than a mighty rolling river being channeled through that person to make all things work together for good. Because of the Holy Spirit, for every believer who prays, all is working together for good. This is sufficient cause for joy.

I Believe in the Holy Spirit

We too easily lose the joy that is ours because we lose sight of the Spirit that is ours when difficulties fill our vision. But our joy cannot be quenched if we put on the spectacles of Scripture to see the working of the Spirit *in* us, *for* us, and *through* us.

When I was in seminary, Professor John Sanderson encouraged every senior who was on the brink of ministry, but who may have been doubting himself, with the account of an experienced minister who had a clear vision of the Holy Spirit's work. The faithful minister served in a historic church where he had to climb a set of steps to the high pulpit. The lofty podium was meant to indicate the importance of the task and the sacredness of the Word that was presented there. Inadvertently, it also made this sensitive servant of God miserably conscious of the inadequacy of his own words. He knew that no eloquence or ability in him could change a human heart or save an eternal soul. The knowledge of his own weakness could have paralyzed him, but he learned to lean on the strength of another. As an affirmation of faith and a petition for power, he breathed a silent prayer as he ascended each step of the pulpit. On each step he said, "I believe in the Holy Spirit, I believe in the Holy Spirit." The words gave him comfort, confidence, and courage, because by them he knew that the effectiveness of his work was not dependent on him.

Since Dr. Sanderson told us of this faithful man of God, I have used his prayer as a pattern for my own ministry. As I approach any pulpit I pray, "I believe in the Holy Spirit, I believe in the Holy Spirit." Years ago I told my wife, Kathy, my habit, but I never realized the impression it made on her until recently.

We were in one of those difficult times in our church, and I determined I must speak on a matter that was very troubling for us all. I worked and worked on that message. I knew I had to say things in just the right way, and ultimately I arranged my words in a form I thought was good. But as I preached that message, nothing I had ever said before seemed to me to be so inadequate, so stumbling, and so unhelpful. The truths I wanted people to grasp felt like sand running through my own fingers.

In the car on the way home I told Kathy how depressed I was because I knew I had failed. I had not been able to say things the way I wanted. The message had not worked. But Kathy did not have the words of consolation I expected. "You are wrong," she said. "That was a tremendous message. It had to be, because in each step as you walked to the pulpit I prayed saying, 'I believe in the Holy Spirit; I believe in the Holy Spirit.'"

Kathy was right. There was still cause for joy, not because of the way I felt, and not because of the way circumstances seemed, but because we trusted the Holy Spirit. Because of the Spirit we have life, sureness of glory, and the promise of good. Christians may fail terribly or face great difficulties, but because the Spirit works in, for, and through them, nothing can steal their joy. Joy pervades their lives because they believe in the Holy Spirit.

QUESTIONS *for Thought*

1. How does the Holy Spirit affect the content of our prayer?
2. How does the Holy Spirit affect the fervency of our prayer?
3. How does the Holy Spirit affect the power of our prayer? How may our attitude toward prayer change when we recognize the Spirit's role?
4. How does your own life have more meaning once you understand the work of the Holy Spirit?

PART THREE

God's Grace

FIVE

The Increase of Grace

I left early one Sunday morning for a preaching assignment that had me driving due east into the morning sun. Because it was early, my eyes, which are normally sensitive to light, reacted even more to the brightness. I had forgotten my sunglasses. Within a half hour my sleeve was drenched from wiping the tears streaming down my face. I knew others were depending on my arrival, so I kept driving despite the blinding light. I pulled the visor down, squinted into the glare, and drove, concentrating on the center line until a truck passed me. That was when I knew I was in trouble. I knew because, though I heard the truck pass me, I never saw it. I quickly steered for the median, braked to a stop, and waited for my sight to return. I made it to my preaching assignment that morning only because of periodic stops along the median where I would duck my head into the shadows beneath my dashboard to let my eyes recuperate from the brightness of the sun.

During one of my shifts under the dashboard I realized I had been blinded by light. Overexposure to what I needed to be able to see had made me unable to see. The verses for this chapter's study of Romans 8 may cause the same results in some of you. If you belong to a church with a heritage strongly tied to the Reformation, these verses are very familiar to you. This passage, which so clearly radiates distinctives of faith dear to our church fathers, is like the morning sun arising over and over again in our services to illumine biblical thought. No verses are cited more often in Sunday school or sermons in efforts to help others see.

Unfortunately, the result of continual journeys into the light of these verses may be the same as my trip into the sun. Overexposure to that which helps us see may actually be blinding. The truths here are so wonderful they may become overwhelming. Still we must travel into this light if we are to complete our trip through this passage. The challenge is to pace our journey and plan our path so that we are not blinded by the light. The words contain too much beauty and warmth to deny ourselves the splendor of their brightness. As dawn's light grows toward day, so *grace increases* as we journey toward the Son.

Romans 8:28–30

[28]And we know that in all things God works for the good of those who love him, who have been called according to his purpose. [29]For those God foreknew he also predestined to be conformed to the likeness of his Son, that he might be the firstborn among many brothers. [30]And those he predestined, he also called; those he called, he also justified; those he justified, he also glorified.

Defining Destinations

"You are what you drive." Do you remember the car commercial that made that insightful psychological observation? I do not know how others reacted to the ad's character analysis, but I found it insulting. Maybe that was because at the time I was driving a vintage Ford Pinto registering over a hundred thousand miles, sporting flaking brown paint, needing new tires, and staining my garage floor with a persistent but undetectable antifreeze leak. I am that? Oh, no!

Actually, I am not very concerned about the ad's claim, because in Romans 8 an entirely different perspective appears. Here I learn that it is not *what* I am driving that characterizes me but *where* I am heading. My destination marks me.

The direction we are going says far more about who we are than what is now taking us there. This is an important realization for every Christian, because too often we evaluate our worth based upon current experience. Either because we are just starting our journey of faith, because we have had some failure in our faith journey, or because we are comparing ourselves with the progress of others on their faith journey, we can feel like vintage Pintos with new Jeep Cherokees zooming past us. We compare others' knowledge with our ignorance; their experience with our mistakes; their apparent piety with our obvious sin—and suddenly, because of what we know we are, we believe ourselves to be worth very little. However, it is not *what* we are, but *where* we are bound that counts with God.

God adds the grace necessary to mark you as his own and to make you after the likeness of his Son. He provides whatever grace is necessary to conform your life to the model of his design. Because your destination is God's own kingdom, you are of infinite value to him, and he provides the grace necessary to make you reflect his own glory. Though your life proceeds along sometimes slippery roads with occasional bumps and even crashes, God adds the grace that keeps you in showroom quality. As your life progresses toward your destination, God continually adds grace to make you shine with the radiance of his glory. This *increase of grace* insures your value to God and assures every Christian of personal worth. As a result, even if you feel like a rusting Pinto, the Bible promises you are more valuable than a new Lexus, because God has chosen to prepare you for himself.

To estimate our worth properly, we must understand the increasing grace that establishes our value. Through this grace, God both *makes* and *marks* us as being as precious as his own Son. This does not mean that we Christians have arrived at perfection, but because we are heading there, we are precious to God despite flaking paint, worn tires, and leaking radiators. By God's grace we have a destination that predetermines our value and guarantees our worth.

The Architecture of God

To understand our worth from God's perspective, we must first see how God makes us valuable to himself. He begins by not settling for the "what is." He is not bound or limited by the conditions he finds in our lives. Like an architect, God sees beyond what is now to what can be. He establishes our value by what he knows he can *make* of us. Our worth is not determined by what characterizes us before God works, or even as he works, but by what will characterize us when his work is done. God is goal oriented.

Not Settling for the "What Is"

A sign recently appeared on the route I jog, announcing a large estate near us would be subdivided for the building of eighteen new homes. The proposal seemed preposterous. Everyone I know who saw the sign also concluded it was crazy to try to build eighteen homes on that land. There was a big lake, lots of trees, and a twisting drive that already swallowed most of the property. We could see no way to fit eighteen homes on the site. But we were not looking with an architect's eye.

The architect knew he did not have to settle for what was there. What made the land valuable to him was not its current condition but what could be done with it. The architect envisioned and evaluated the land without the limitations of its current conditions. He did not settle for the "what is" but planned for what could be. The same is true of God as he looks at us. He considers our value in the light of what he plans to make us rather than on the basis of what we are. God is not limited by current conditions; therefore, our value is not fixed by what is or has been true of us.

These familiar verses of Romans 8 are important for Christians who question their worth, because here Paul puts God's spiritual architecture on display. By seeing how God builds, Christians can understand why they are valuable to God despite the sin and weaknesses of their current condition. Their limitations do not thwart God's plans for their development and thus do not depreciate their worth. The architectural images help them understand God's perspective with terms familiar to anyone who has been involved in a building program.

Any building program begins with selection of a site and the formulation of a plan for use of the site. God's spiritual building program begins the same way. The apostle says, "Those God foreknew he also predestined to be conformed to the likeness of his Son" (v. 29). Here is *site selection* and *site planning*. God does not just start building arbitrarily or randomly. He "foreknows" where, or in whom, he will work. A site is chosen. Then the plans for that site are stated. God determines to conform that individual to the likeness of his Son. This design indicates God intends to develop a person modeled after his Son. Jesus is not to be the only child of God's love. He is to be the firstborn of many brothers (v. 29). God plans many similar developments.

To carry out his plans to conform others to the holy image of his Son, God cannot be limited to the conditions he finds at the sites he works. Therefore, Paul explains how God executes his plan. Those God predestines to be conformed to the likeness of his Son, are "called," "justified," and "glorified" (v. 30). These are important words for the process of spiritual construction, which has received careful preparation in this chapter of Romans.

God's "call" is the work of *site preparation*. Nothing can be built in most communities in this country without numerous phone calls to prepare for the building process. One must call contractors, suppliers, zoning boards, building inspectors, lawyers, city officials, and many others before the site can be developed. When we call any one of these parties, we send our voice across telephone lines so others will respond to our needs. When God "calls" us, he sends his Word by his Spirit into our hearts so we can respond to him. If the calling of the Holy Spirit did not occur, no spiritual development could proceed. Our hearts would be cold, hard, and hostile to God if the Spirit did not work to prepare them for the development God intends (see vv. 7–9). The Spirit warms our hearts toward the Father so that we can accept God's plans. How appropriate it is to say that we are "called," that God sends his voice into our hearts by his Spirit to prepare us for the work he will do at that site.

Once all the approvals for construction are secured, building still cannot proceed without *site clearing*. The area flagged for construction must be cleared of all barriers and debris. Before construction of the eighteen homes on the former estate near us began, the builder straightened the twisting drive. He removed excess trees. He even moved the lake. The land was cleared of every hindrance to the new construction.

Spiritual construction requires a similar wiping away of past problems. The apostle describes God's spiritual site-clearing process by saying that those whom God called he also "justified" (v. 30). Romans 8 provides for a rich understanding of the term's meaning. God clears our hearts by pardoning our pasts and wiping away the sinful garbage. "Therefore, there is now no condemnation for those who are in Christ Jesus," because God spared not his own Son but made him a sin offering for us (see vv. 1–3, 32). God clears our lives of the guilt of sin to build a new life in the likeness of his Son.

After the land is cleared, the builder constructs the *final edifice*. The developer ultimately completed those eighteen homes on the site of the old estate near our home. In a similar fashion, after God clears our hearts of guilt, he also completes his work in us. Paul says those God justified, he also glorified (v. 30). The apostle describes the wonder of God's completed work by saying the difficulties of this life cannot be compared with what will be revealed in us when we are fully redeemed, body and spirit, as children of the living God (vv. 18–23). This is God's ultimate structure—the house made without hands, reserved in heaven for us (see 2 Cor. 5:1; 1 Peter 1:4). When God finishes his construction, each believer reflects the glorious image of God's Son, Jesus Christ. When we are glorified, we are with the Father and like the Son. This construction is not finished yet—and will not be until Christ's return—but the final product is so glorious and so evident to the eye of faith that its worth is sure (Rom. 8:24–25).

Christian under Construction

With the apostle Paul's guidance we can see the spiritual architecture of site preparation, site clearing, and final edifice in the believer's calling, justification, and glorification. But something appears to be missing. Paul's description seems to jump from land clearing to building completion. Where is the *building process?*

Paul is too careful a writer, and the Lord is too precise an architect, to fail to describe so crucial a phase of construction. The process of conforming believers more and more to the likeness of Jesus, which is ordinarily called sanctification, has been described in detail. Our eyes may simply have skimmed over the specifications because of over-familiarity with the words. When Paul says God works all together for good to them that love him and are called according to his purpose (v. 28), we are not left to guess what "good" or "purpose" he is talking about. God's ultimate good and purpose for each of us is to conform us to the likeness of Jesus so that we might call him our brother (v. 30). Our Father works all things toward this family purpose and allows nothing in our lives except what makes us more like Jesus. This is the Christian construction process.

When the construction began on the estate near us, the builder placed a large fence around the property. He allowed nothing through the gate except what aided the development of the new homes. In the process of sanctification God fences our lives with his purpose and allows nothing to enter except that which develops us more into the image of Christ Jesus.

The circle of God's care is one of the Christian's greatest comforts. It assures us nothing enters our lives except that which is working for an ultimate good. The circle does not mean all things seem good or are easy, but it does insure no occurrence is purposeless or senseless. God allows nothing except what will conform us more to the likeness of Jesus and will transform our world in accord with his purposes. Not all is immediately good (there is much cruelty and tragedy in this fallen world), but God works all for a greater good. This does not always make things easy, but it makes difficulties bearable and gives us a perspective on trials that keeps despair distant.

God's construction process is meant to give you hope as well as endurance as a believer. If all that enters your life conforms you more to the likeness of Jesus, as long as you live, God constructs you to be like his own Son. God is still not settling for the "what is." Because things keep happening in your life, God is still building. As long as you live, God works. He wiped away the debris from your past and destined a glorious future for you, but he also improves on you right now. Each new event in your life is an addition of grace. As long as things keep entering your life, grace keeps increasing. The heavenly builder is making you more than you are. In fact, because God surrounds all us believers with his purposes, we all are on the way to becoming more than we are.

Unburdened and Unshackled

A wonderful assurance to Christian believers is knowing they are not bound to past sins or present failures. Because God has wiped out the past, has prepared the future, and works in the present to change them more into Christ's likeness, they need never fear their esteem is shackled to what they regret. Believers are released from the shame that devalues them in their own eyes, because their ultimate worth is not determined by what they were or what they are.

One of my best friends when I briefly attended college in Tennessee was a young Christian whom I fear may never have learned the relief of release from his own regrets. He was a premed student named Samuel. Premeds at major universities are an intense bunch. The competition for the grades needed to qualify for medical school requires fine minds and hard work. Despite the pressures, Samuel was doing just fine until he returned from summer vacation after his junior year.

Though his grades stayed high, Samuel talked as though he was beginning to doubt himself. Self-deprecating comments became habitual as he downgraded his potential to be a doctor. Ultimately he drove himself into a deep depression. One night Samuel came back to the dorm having had too much to drink. This too was very unlike him. Something was eating at him, and that night, in his unguarded state, he told what it was.

Samuel is a black man from Alabama. The summer before his senior year he went home from college. Driving late at night on a rural road, he came across an accident. A car had crashed through a guard rail into a deep culvert. The man inside could not move.

Samuel knew enough from his premed course work to realize the man's back was probably broken. He raced to the nearest farm house to get help. When he knocked, an older white woman came to the door. She was obviously scared of Samuel, but he pleaded with her to call an ambulance. She listened to his frantic pleas through a chain-latched door, but eventually seemed convinced he was telling the truth. She turned away as if to make the phone call, then hesitated and cracked the door again to ask a question. By her tone Samuel realized the answer would determine if she would complete the call.

The woman asked, "Is the injured man black or is he white?"

The question sent Samuel reeling. A lifetime of growing up under racial prejudice as a highly intelligent and sensitive black man suddenly exploded in him. The degree of inhumanity evident in a question so laden with insult and bigotry toward another human being enraged him. An anger fed by a lifetime of discrimination boiled in him and poured from his lips with a vehemence of which he had not known himself capable. Samuel shouted, "He's white, and now he's your problem."

Then Samuel left. He did not just leave the farm house, he drove from the area and never looked back. He was true to his angry words. He left the accident scene and the injured man for others to find. In his anger at inhumanity, my gentle friend became as monstrous as the bigotry he hated. Though he was preparing to be a doctor, Samuel drove away, leaving a man hurt and possibly dying. Now it haunted him. Samuel's future, the value he placed on himself, his anticipated achievements, his potential to serve others—all were shackled to the weight of a past act from which he could not now unchain himself. It pulled him down into despair, because deep in his heart he believed his failure now characterized him. He lost hope in his future, because he believed he could not be free of his past.

Believers need never fear such despair. The Bible says God is the lifter of our heads. He takes no delight in bowing us down with the shame of our pasts. We may be guilty of terrible failures, but God has freed us from guilt by sending his Son to bear the penalty we deserve. Having justified us, God does not hold confessed sin over us. He refuses to burden us again. Instead he puts new hope in our vision of ourselves by telling us he will continue to sanctify our lives so that we will more and more reflect his Son, in preparation for the time when we will be with him in glory. Past failures do not characterize us anymore. Nothing is more true of us than what God intends for us to be. Because God is the architect of our futures, his plan for us is far more certain than the implications of our pasts. Our worth is determined by the glorious future God foreknows (v. 29), rather than by a shameful past we would like to forget.

Washed Down Higher

Christians have a glorious future regardless of sin in the past or shortcomings in the present. Despite what we are or have been, we are destined for higher purposes because of God's work. He cleanses us of confessed sin to build us to greater heights of holiness and to bring us closer to his glory.

The mounds of sand at the Great Sand Dunes National Park in Colorado peak at over nine hundred feet. On those hills people really do look like ants. Though the height of the dunes is spectacular, there is as much wonder contained in their formation. The Medano River flows through the lower dunes washing tons of sand into a mountain valley below. One would expect the water to erode the dunes away over time or at least to shrink them a bit. However, the valley into which the river washes the sand is between two mountain ranges that funnel the winds into a nearly continuous gale blowing back toward the dunes. The more the river washes, the more sand the winds carry to build the dunes even higher. In the same manner, as God washes our sin away, he does not lessen our significance. He washes us to raise our spirits to new heights of holiness. God washes and builds in a continuing process of grace, lifting us higher and higher toward himself.

You may fear that even as a Christian you are insignificant. Others may seem to have better backgrounds than you or to have more knowledge than you or to have the gifts you want. Some may seem to have conquered the sins you are still fighting. You may recognize you have taken some wrong turns or fear a wreck ahead. All Christians face similar fears and hurts. But we will despair only if we forget that our past is wiped away and that our present is not our future. God is not limited to using us as we are. He is not done with us yet. He is conforming each of our lives to his glorious purpose, making us more like Jesus.

Because the builder is divine, we need not fear that the final project will fail. God is the engineer. We may begin as cluttered and unlovely, but we are all beautifully constructed and landscaped by the time God is finished. Grace increases until God's work is done.

 **QUESTIONS** *for Thought*

1. How does God use an architect's eye to determine the value of those he loves?
2. What comfort is it that God is not settling for the "what is" in our lives?
3. How does God insure that we are all on the road to being more than we are?
4. How does knowing our final destination and ultimate value make our lives better now?

SIX

The Mystery of Grace

I wrote the end of the last chapter about God's work of increasing grace intending to encourage, but I realize some may be discouraged by the concepts. Almost all of us appreciate the fact that God increases our value as he forgives our weaknesses. But to acknowledge the continuing process, we must confess its incompleteness. If grace must still increase, then we are not finished products. We have a glorious destination, but we have not yet arrived.

If we confess we have not arrived, our value may seem diminished even in our own eyes. How can we avoid feeling reduced in worth if we must confess that we are not all God intends us to be? The apostle answers by reminding us that we are not valuable simply because of where we are destined; we are valuable because we *are* our destination.

Paul must have known how discouraged we could be by thinking that our full potential, and thus our full value, lies out in the future somewhere. So Paul captures our imaginations and comforts our hearts with a word puzzle, the solution of which confirms our present value to God. By solving the gentle mystery, we understand that God not only *makes* us valuable, he has already *marked* our full worth.

Forward into the Past

We know our ultimate worth to God when we consider his architectural assessment. The validity of all property assessments is related to the time of appraisal. Paul's assessment of our spiritual worth also contains key time elements. He first explains how the divine builder is working on us now, stating that God is working all things together for good (v. 28). This *present* activity is adding to our value. Next Paul explains our worth in terms of our background. He says, those "God foreknew he also predestined to be conformed to the image of Jesus" (v. 29). Here Paul uses the *past* tense, because foreknowledge and predestination are actions of our architect that relate to previous site planning (see Eph. 1:4, 5).

As the apostle continues his description of God's work, the puzzle of the tenses develops (Rom. 8:30). At first there is no hint of mystery. Paul uses the *past* tense, saying God called us, because God's saving call is a past action for everyone who is now a believer. The same is true of God's work of salvation, so Paul again uses the *past* tense to say we have been justified. The mystery unfolds when Paul uses this same *past* tense to describe a *future* state. He says, "those God justified, he also glorified." The only glory that Paul has described for us believers in this chapter is that time at which we are spiritually and physically redeemed when creation itself is renewed (see vv. 18–23). This glorification is undoubtedly in the future. How, then, can Paul characterize it in the *past* tense? The mystery is solved in realizing our final glory is so certain that Paul is able to state it as an accomplished fact. Paul states a future reality as a past act because its certainty makes it as definite as if it had already happened.

Fixed Regard and Firm Relationships

The key to understanding this mystery is in grasping the full implications of the fact that God "foreknew" each believer (v. 29). If I already know all about something before I have contact with it, I likely have an opinion about it. Fritz Rienecker, the language expert, says to foreknow means "to fix the regard" one has about something or someone. If I am invited to the cinema and I say, "I already know all about that movie," I imply more than that I simply know what the show is about. I cannot say, "I know what that movie will be like," without in some sense indicating I have already assessed its value. By indicating foreknowledge about something, I signal I have determined its worth to me.

When we foreknow something, we fix our regard for it. Because our foreknowledge is fallible, we make mistakes. Not so, God. His knowledge is in accord with what he will accomplish as the divine architect. So when he fixes his regard for us, the value he places on us is entirely accurate.

In more personal terms, to foreknow is to determine the relationship one will have with another. In the Scriptures, knowledge often refers to a relational bond. The Bible says that Adam *knew* his wife and she gave birth to a son. Elsewhere the apostle Paul says, "He made Him who *knew* no sin to be sin for us" (2 Cor. 5:21 NKJV). Now, of course, Jesus knew about sin, but he had no relationship or union with sin. However, if God foreknows someone, he already has an essential and proper relationship with that person. For God to foreknow us means he has established his relationship with us. What is God's relationship with those he foreknows? Paul states the answer clearly: Those God foreknew he predestined to be like Jesus so that Jesus would be the first of many brothers (Rom. 8:29).

God regards us as his family. He relates to us just as he does to his own child, because he knows we will be like Jesus. He has fixed his regard for us. He considers us as precious as his own Son. When he looks at us he sees Jesus. Our glory is predetermined because we are foreknown.

Glory (heaven) is our destination, but we are our destination because we are already glorious to our God. Paul echoes this idea elsewhere, writing that when God saved us he "raised us up with Christ and seated us with him in the heavenly realms" (Eph. 2:6). Our heavenly position is already ratified. God has already seated us in glory. We "have arrived" in terms of the regard God has for us. We are already enthroned as full members of the kingdom, "heirs of God and co-heirs with Christ" (Rom. 8:17). How can this be? Because God has foreknown us and thus fixed his regard for us.

All the Love There Is

What are the practical ramifications of God's foreknowledge? One is our wonderful assurance that even if we feel undeserving, we know we are regarded as glorious Christians by God. We are already of infinite value to God, as precious to him as his own Son. This means we are already loved as fully as we can be. We cannot do anything to gain more of God's love, because we already have all the love there is to have.

Some people are defeated in their Christian lives because they think they must continually earn God's affection. They are weighed down by the perception that they must keep striving to fulfill the never-ending task of satisfying the righteous demands of a never-to-be-satisfied God. The truth is our best works are but filthy rags to God (Isa. 64:6). Our acceptance is always totally dependent on his grace (Eph. 2:8–9). We cannot do anything to gain more of God's affection, but because God has fixed his regard for us as his own children, we do not despair. We will never be loved any more by God, and we can be loved no less, for God already loves us as he loves his own Son who resides in us. We have all of God's love.

"Oh," but you say, "I sin." Yes, but grace increases. God covers your sin and keeps loving you. Like oil in the jar of the widow of Zarephath (1 Kings 17), the more grace God pours, the more it increases. But you ask, "Doesn't God punish sin? Doesn't he get angry at my unrepentance?" Yes, this is true. Still, you must understand that God only disciplines to prevent you from persisting in sin that endangers you. Discipline does not deny his love. What father does not seek to turn a child from danger or to discourage him from actions that will lead to greater hurt? The Scriptures say, "the Lord disciplines those he loves" (Heb. 12:6). That means that even when you are being disciplined, God is only driving you away from danger and drawing you closer to himself. In the throes of his greatest chastening, you are never loved more.

The Bible says, "He who will not discipline his child, hates his child." God says, "I love you enough to discipline you." But when he says, "This hurts me more than it does you," he really means it. Your sin required the sacrifice of his Son. Your sanctification requires that he look past the suffering of his own Son to care for the person who caused it. Yes, cavalier sin angers and hurts God, but his pain is never more intense than his compassion. His love is greater than your sin. His wrath, the product of a deeper love, smolders at the hurt you do to yourself. As a loving parent is enraged by the life-threatening carelessness of a teenager oblivious to his own mortality, God's anger flashes because damage is being done to one so dear to him. His discipline is never the sign of rejection; it is the mark of your preciousness to God. Only his carelessness would allow you to persist in sin. When you have experienced the wrath of God, do not doubt his care. To fear the discipline of the Father is right and proper, but to question the love of his motives is never appropriate. When you believe you have been knocked down, remember God is still in your corner. No matter what you feel, he is always lifting you up. How else will you be able to get up?

When Down Is Up

Driving through the mountains of Colorado on a family vacation, we discovered how easy it is to mistake an up for a down. We drove through an extremely difficult mountain pass. Mountains on both sides arched away from the car at amazing angles and seemed by their very magnitude to force us down. Yet despite our visual sensation of traveling downward, the struggling noise of our car engine indicated we were climbing up. A look in the rearview mirror cleared our understanding. By focusing on where we had been rather than on the craggy heights, we realized that the mountains we were climbing created the optical illusion of going down while we were really climbing higher. In the same way, when we face difficulties and discipline we often feel we are being borne down, but over time a backward look will reveal that God lifts us only higher and higher. God leads his own closer to himself because they are precious to him.

God's actions teach us we must be careful not to make believers fear the rejection of God. If anyone must climb to his favor, we shall all fall. If we have to win our way back into his affection, we are all lost. If his regard for us is not fixed, we will never win his affection. We still have only rags to woo him. To turn believers from sin on the basis of God's rejection is to create bitter, hard, prideful people, but not more godly people. A biblical view of the unlimited, unchanging love of God is the only path to healthy holiness. Unless the love of Christ constrains us to do his will, our hearts will be no closer to God even if our behaviors change. There is no incentive to climb closer to God unless we are sure his love will not let us go. His Word assures us we will not fall, because his affection for us is fixed.

Much Scripture becomes clear and comforting when we recognize that God's regard for believers is fixed. We begin to understand why there is so much emphasis on Christ's work as our only hope of salvation or divine favor. Our value is based solely on the work of Christ that marks us as God's children. Our own works, fraught with human weakness and sin, never could make us acceptable to God nor sure of his favor. But because our own works are not what make us acceptable to God, we do not fear that his love is as fragile, or as likely to fail, as our holiness. By grace we are freed of working to win God's favor. Perhaps this is why the Bible says that when we become Christians we enter into a holy *rest* (Heb. 4:3). The struggle for God's affection is over. We *rest* from our labors and now pursue God's work. The church fathers said we believers "receive and *rest* upon Christ alone for our salvation." The hymnist writes, "I *rest* me in the thought, I am his and he is mine forever and forever." What joy, what peace, what strength are ours knowing we have all the love there is to have and nothing will change that. We are able to serve our God with full vigor because we are well rested.

The End from the Beginning

One of the men I most respect is my father-in-law. An event in his life still teaches me much about the importance of knowing our eternal worth. Bob raised a fine family (including a pretty fair daughter), sacrificially provided for the welfare of aging relatives for many years, and loyally labored as an engineer for one company all his working life. All these are wonderful accomplishments, but Bob's crowning achievement is his house. By himself Bob built the large two-story house with a full basement, two-car garage, and adjoining guest house for an invalid relative.

I do not mean what those of us in modern suburbia imply when I say Bob "built" a house. He did not have a contractor build a home to his specifications. My father-in-law used his hammer, his saw, and his two hands to build his own house. He is a real craftsman. And seeing the result, I cannot help but hold him in high regard, as does the rest of his family.

One of the nifty features of the house is a stairway that turns twice—first off the entry hall and then up to the second floor. The stairway looks great now, but my wife says she has never seen more frustration in her dad's eyes than when he built those stairs. As a craftsman, Bob would settle for no prefab staircase. The tricky angles and cuts caused by the turns in the stairs he figured out by himself—but not the first time.

He bought a load of lumber, measured each step, marked the board, sawed it, and fit each step. That is, he tried to fit each step. The task turned out to be a bit trickier than he anticipated and required every ounce of his ingenuity. By that afternoon he had to go back to the lumberyard to get another load of lumber. He measured, marked, sawed, and tried to fit again. By nightfall the stairs were still not right, and it looked as if there might be another trip to the lumberyard. Recalling the moment, my wife says her father turned his back on those stairs, walked out to the front yard in utter frustration, and hung his head in tearful shame. He felt defeated, embarrassed, and worthless as the craftsman he wanted to be. But what if Bob had known the end from the beginning? What if he had known it was all going to turn out good? What if he had known that our regard for him would not change one iota despite this failure of the moment? In fact, because we now know the challenge of the task, our regard for him increases. We are aware of what a true achievement the final product is. If Bob had known our regard for him would be fixed at the highest level, then the task may not have gotten easier, but his strength, his resolve, and his joy in the certainty of his success would have granted him encouragement for the completion of his work.

The Lord knows we sometimes are not the Christians we should be or even want to be. We get frustrated, make mistakes, and have not yet completed all the steps we need to climb. This knowledge of our failings could deflate us, weaken us, or defeat us. So God gives us this great lesson on his increasing grace. He tells us the end from the beginning. He says, "I do not look at you, child, on the basis of what you are, but on the basis of where you are going. You are not limited to what you are. I am making you more than you are, adding to you what you need to finish my work. Because of what you will be, I already have fixed you in my heart as precious. When I look at you, I see only my glorious child, because I have destined you to be like Jesus."

Believer, because of God's increasing grace, you are already valued in accord with your destination. You are predestined to be conformed to the likeness of Jesus, that he might be the firstborn among many brothers (v. 29).

God tells you the end from the beginning so that your joy may be full all along the way.

 **QUESTIONS** *for Thought*

1. Does not yet being a "finished product" of God sometimes discourage you? Why?
2. How does God's foreknowledge of what you will be affect your preciousness to him today?
3. Why is God's discipline not a sign of his rejection?
4. How does God's fixed regard for you affect your assessment of your own worth—even when you fail?

SEVEN

The Perseverance of Grace

A s our family walked a nature trail on a recent trip, we came to a tree identified as a limber pine. Our guidebook said the tree got its name from the unusual flexibility of its limbs. The branches are so limber that a person can tie a knot in them as though each limb were a thick strand of rope. The guidebook invited us to test this quality by tying a knot in one of the limbs ourselves. Our children clamored for the opportunity to tie a knot in a tree. Unfortunately, the branches were higher than the children could reach, and the hundreds of nature walkers who had preceded us over the years had already knotted every branch within adult reach. The only way our children could tie their knots was by letting me hold them as high as I could to first unknot each branch they wanted to tie. The children succeeded in unknotting the branches because they managed to reach as high as those who first tied the knots. But imagine how difficult their task would have been if the knots had been made at the top of the tree. Imagine how impossible their task if the knots had been tied in heaven.

A knot made in heaven would be impossible for my children to untie. Once God has bound us to his love, it is just as impossible for God's children to untie that knot secured in heaven. God's promise of peace, the life-changing work of the Holy Spirit, and the continuing provision of grace are works of heaven that bind us to God. Since God secures the knot of grace that binds us to him, it will persevere against the pressures that threaten to loose it. A knot tied by men could be undone, but a knot made by God is beyond man's reach and invulnerable to this world's unraveling tensions. This is why church fathers in many different traditions have said we can count on God's grace to last as long as we live. Because God's grace alone unites us with him, we can expect *perseverance therein to the end.* This expectation is not the result of logical speculation or optimistic wishing; it is the promise of Scripture.

Romans 8:28–30; 38–39

[28]And we know that in all things God works for the good of those who love him, who have been called according to his purpose. [29]For those God foreknew he also predestined to be conformed to the likeness of his Son, that he might be the firstborn among many brothers. [30]And those he predestined, he also called; those he called, he also justified; those he justified, he also glorified.

[38]For I am convinced that neither death nor life, neither angels nor demons, neither the present nor the future, nor any powers, [39]neither height nor depth, nor anything else in all creation, will be able to separate us from the love of God that is in Christ Jesus our Lord.

The Cliff

She is thirty-three. Her husband, a minister, ran off with the church organist eighteen months ago. The worst of the pain, the shock, and the court dates are all over. It is time to close that chapter of life, to try to collect one's self, and to move on. But she cannot. She cannot seem to resolve to do anything.

Someone suggests she talk with a pastor, and she does. When she speaks to him, it is not about anger, not about depression, not about guilt. She speaks of fear. She says, "I don't know if I can trust myself. I thought my husband had it all together. I worshiped him for the faith I thought he had. I still don't know anyone who knows more about God and the Bible. If now he says he's not a Christian, how do I know I will be? I'm scared to step forward in any direction. What if the same cliff over which he fell is out there waiting for me, and somewhere, someday, I'm going to fall off it too?"

The questions are not easy, but they are real. They are the cry of uncertainty in a world where trauma and sin may converge to cause believers to wonder if they are secure in God's love. So pressing are the questions that theologians in all traditions have been forced to answer in some way. Some talk about "eternal security," or about "the security of believers." In my church we speak of "the perseverance of the saints" to express the biblical truth of God's abiding care for all believers. Regardless of the terminology or faith tradition, this truth by any name tastes sweet when life is so bitter that it casts doubt on whether we shall endure in God's love. God's promises of perseverance are the wonderful reassurances that because the knot of salvation securing us to God is tied by him, no one and nothing can undo it. The faith that is genuine is perpetual.

We do not have to worry that there is a cliff of sin or circumstance out there somewhere that might cause us to fall away from God, because he is the one who guides our paths and upholds us with his everlasting arms. Perseverance is the great assurance that will keep us fearlessly striding forward in our faith.

Proofs of Perseverance

Not all agree that the knot of salvation cannot be untied and that there is such a thing as perseverance of the saints. Therefore, it is important to examine Scripture for what proofs it offers. All our theologizing is fruitless if God's Word does not affirm our thought. All our counsel is false comfort if our answers are not echoed by God.

The Domino Effect

Perhaps the most cited proof of the perseverance of grace is Romans 8:29–30. The process of salvation is described here in a way that seems to assure us that God's grace secures eternally if it begins at all. The apostle says that those God foreknows he predestines, those he predestines he calls, those he calls he justifies, those he justifies he glorifies. "Look," we say, "these descriptions are just like dominoes falling in sequence. Those foreknown are the ones predestined; those predestined the same as those called; those called the same as those justified; and those justified are the very ones who will be glorified. When God tips the first domino in the process of salvation the final results are certain." We conclude that all those truly justified—which is to say, all true believers—are heaven bound. No exceptions.

Not all believers agree that this text teaches that Christians have an unending and unseverable relationship with their God. Christians of another perspective reply, "Those glorified surely have been justified, but this does not exclude the possibility that some of those justified may not reach glory. These verses certainly describe the pattern for those who ultimately reach heaven, but some may have fallen along the way. Simply because all adults were once children does not mean all children become adults." This opinion does not seem to deal adequately with the text, which explicitly says," *those* he justified, *those* [i.e., the very same] God glorified." The apostle seems to make the point that the persons first cited comprise the group cited secondly. No subsidiary group is indicated to have fallen out of the persons first mentioned. In fact, the language pointedly indicates the two groups are the same.

The past tense the apostle uses in these verses emphasizes the security of believers because, as noted in the previous chapter of this book, it indicates a *fait accompli*. Once God justifies, the believer is already glorified, from heaven's perspective. The reason the passage indicates justified persons comprise the group of glorified persons is that the two groups are the same already. In this context, were Paul even to imply that those who are justified might not fully comprise the group glorified, he would be indicating that God removes glorified saints from heaven. Such a likelihood seems remote. But simply because we may not consider the argument valid does not mean it is without advocates.

The Unbreakable Bond

Some persons who perceive the need to promote holiness among believers through fear of divine rejection insist they can sever their relationship with God. The motive of producing holiness is noble, but the argument must still be rejected if it is out of accord with God's Word. The verses that conclude Romans 8 indicate that threats of divine rejection do not harmonize with heaven's song. Following reassurances that believers are not condemned by God because of the sacrifice of Christ (vv. 31–37), Paul practically sings the beautiful assurance they have of God's unending love. He says:

> [38]I am convinced that neither death nor life, neither angels nor demons, neither the present nor the future, nor any powers, [39]neither height nor depth, nor anything else in all creation, will be able to separate us from the love of God that is in Christ Jesus our Lord.

Paul seems nearly to exhaust the imagination identifying circumstances others will label as sufficient to indicate God no longer loves those he has redeemed with the blood of his own Son. But Paul's conclusion is the same for each anticipated circumstance: "Nothing in all creation can break the bond of love that unites us to God through the work of Jesus."

Christians with other perspectives still may not be convinced, despite the emphasis of Paul's words. Often they reply, "Yes, none of *these* things can separate us from God, but there's something not mentioned in that list." What is it? Sin. They argue, "Personal sin can still separate us from God." It is true that sin is not directly mentioned in the list. But sin and sinners are both part of creation. If Paul says that nothing in all creation can separate us from the love of God, then surely personal sin does not sever the divine bond that holds us. My mistakes do not tie the hands of the God who has determined to hold me (see John 6:39; 10:28).

The Clincher

Now do not abandon hope of resolving these issues, and please do not feel frustrated when Christians differ. Faithful members of God's family argue about matters dear to them only when they are concerned for each other. Behind the discussion is compassion, commitment to comfort correctly, and a deep desire to know God's intent. That is why the last verse to consider in this discussion is so critical. More clearly than any other, it addresses God's ultimate will and thus highlights how sure we can be of his abiding affection for us despite past or potential failures. The key verse is the one that opens this paragraph of thought, Romans 8:28: "And we know that in all things God works for the good of those who love him, who have been called according to his purpose." Some may object that this verse can hardly be the key, since it contains no explicit mention of perseverance, but such a conclusion is premature.

Consider what treasures lie beneath the surface of this familiar verse. The apostle says God works all things together for the good of those who love him. Who can love God? Only those made alive by the Spirit who are not hostile to God (vv. 7–8). Thus, God works all things together for the good of true believers, that is, those in whom his Spirit has worked. But what is the "good" Paul is talking about? We know the apostle does not say all things seem good or pleasant or nice, because he has just reminded us of the believer's sufferings in this life (v. 18). The "good" Paul says God accomplishes refers to an ultimate good. That ultimate purpose is understood when Paul's thought is followed into subsequent verses: "All works together for good. . . . [F]or those God foreknew he predestined to be conformed to the image of His Son." The "good" God accomplishes makes us more like Jesus.

God is working all things for the ultimate good of conforming us to the likeness of Jesus Christ. Because of our humanity and sin the process is not always steady. It may seem to include large and lengthy setbacks as God allows each individual to learn necessary lessons about personal weakness and divine mercy, which ultimately prepare us to reign with Christ. The lessons are drafted with incredible specificity of design and care for each personality. God alone knows what must be done to form the complexities of human nature into his Son's likeness. None of us actually achieves full form until we are with the Lord, because only there are we fully able to see how gracious God has been to us despite our sin. In the full apprehension of the love of God that held us despite our weakness is the ultimate humility through which actual Christ-likeness is achieved. Perhaps the reason God lets some persist in sin so long is that he knows how deep is the humility required for those personalities to become Christ-like when from their perspective in heaven they see how gracious he has been to them.

No Breath beyond Belief

Because God has promised to work for our ultimate good, we cannot be destined for heaven one day and bound for hell the next. Were it even possible for us to make some decision or take some action that would deny us heaven tomorrow, then an all-knowing God would have to take us there today. Our ultimate good would never allow God even to let us live until a tomorrow that would lead to hell. In the hymn "O Sacred Head Now Wounded," we sing the prayer, "Oh, let me never, never outlive my love to thee." A God concerned about our ultimate good must answer this petition.

God will not allow us to draw one breath beyond belief. If we were about to indulge in some unpardonable sin or engage in some unforgivable lifestyle, then in terms of our ultimate good it would be better that God take us now than lose us forever. It would be far better for us to die and enter heaven early than live to enter hell eternally. It would be far better to lose a few moments from the life the Bible says is only a handbreadth of eternal time (Ps. 39:5) than to live the full span of earth's existence only to inherit the pains of hell forever. No one's ultimate good could be served by living to the point that they are no longer God's. If God knew we were going to untie the knot of our salvation, his love would require that he deny us the opportunity. If we are God's, we shall be God's throughout this life, because he who gave his Son for us could not allow us to live a day that, in his foreknowledge, he knew would destine us to hell. Because God must be true to his Word when he says he is working all for good, believers shall persevere in his grace to the end.

A Parent's Care

The ultimate good heaven offers is one of our greatest sources of comfort. My wife and I saw this vividly when we recently visited a dear friend. Only weeks before, her teenage daughter, a beautiful young Christian, had been killed in a farming accident. The young girl had been helping an older brother bring cows to a milk barn. A cow stumbled and fell against some heavy equipment which toppled onto the girl.

The apparent senselessness of the tragedy made it all the more difficult to bear. But this mother's grief did not blind her to the promises of her God. With a deep faith in God's ultimate goodness, she told us how she had been stirred to talk back to a television ad after her daughter was killed. It was a public service announcement cautioning young people to say no to illegal drugs. The ad began by depicting the nightmare to which drugs can lead. When she saw the scene, this faithful mother stood up, shook her finger at the TV, and said to the world of pain it represented, "You can't get my Sally. She is with the Lord. You can't touch her. My baby is safe now!"

In the midst of her terrible hurt this Christian mother claimed the ultimate good that even death could not deny her daughter. Her daughter is beyond the threats of this world's nightmares, because she has been delivered to the place of endless day. Sally had not been about to enter a world of drug abuse prior to her death. Her radiant Christian testimony was evident to all. Nevertheless, she faced the future threats to godliness that challenge all young people in our culture today. In the senseless horror of Sally's death, there was still comfort for her mother in the knowledge that her daughter is now safe from all threats. If an earthly mother takes solace in the ultimate grace that now guards her daughter from potential dangers in this world, how much more zealous must our heavenly Father be to provide an ultimate good that rescues his children from the sure dangers of hell.

If God's love is real and if his Word is true (as both are), then he could never allow a child of his own to walk forward into hell when heaven stands only a denied heartbeat away. Life is not so sweet that a heavenly Father would permit his children to savor its continuance to the point that it became poison to their souls. Were it even possible for believers to abandon their salvation (see Matt. 24:24), God would never abandon his responsibilities to provide for their ultimate good. Because the God who holds our lives in his hands has the heart of a father, we shall persevere in his grace until the end that secures his love forever.

QUESTIONS
for Thought

1. How might fear of God's rejection stimulate holiness? How might such fear deprive us of holiness?
2. How does God's activity in saving us affect our understanding of how secure is our salvation?
3. What keeps us from using the promises of persevering grace to abuse God's love?
4. Why would it be against God's nature to let a true Christian draw one breath beyond belief?

EIGHT

The Purposes of Perseverance

Our eternal security is not a matter for idle speculation. God does not provide for our perseverance in his grace because he delights in hearing the theologians debate it. Grace is for our good. By understanding God's intentions we may deepen our appreciation for his love and grow in gratitude for his work in our hearts. God has not left us to guess about these intentions. While assuring us of the proofs of God's persevering grace, Romans 8 also indicates the purposes of perseverance.

Promotes Holiness

Perseverance promotes holiness. This may seem to be a controversial claim even among certain advocates of perseverance. Often the Bible's statements on perseverance are characterized as meaning once saved, always saved. This characterization is then interpreted by others to mean, "Now that my ticket to heaven is stamped, sin city, here I come in the meantime." If these characterizations are correct, then surely no holiness is promoted by perseverance. Perseverance that invites evil indulgence with impunity does not encourage piety.

There is no incentive for righteousness once you are saved if perseverance is just a fancy way of saying godliness is now unnecessary. The question is whether such an interpretation of perseverance is correct. Would Scripture ever teach that which invites sin? The interpretive questions are not new. History records that while in prison awaiting a trial that could result in a death sentence, Puritan leader John Bunyan argued with fellow prisoners whether assurance of heaven promoted holiness or granted license.

The ancientness of the debate might seem to give us scant hope of finding real answers. But the age-old questions are actually moot on the basis of this passage. Consider the precise wording (see v. 28). Who will persevere in God's grace? Those for whom God works all things for ultimate good. Who are those persons? *Those who love God!* The promise of perseverance applies only to those whose hearts beat for God. Attitude or actions that say, "Now that I am covered by the shed blood of Jesus Christ, I will take advantage of God, use his grace, manipulate his affections, and abuse the sacrifice of his Son," disclose no real love for God. "Have perseverance, will party" cannot be defended from Scripture, because perseverance is promised only to those whose love for God is genuine.

True affection for God results in the desire to please him. Love for God, which is requisite for the application of God's perseverance promise, is evidenced by the pursuit of the purposes of his calling. Thus, the *assurance* of perseverance applies only to those persevering in love for God and faithfulness to his purposes. Willingly to sin on the assumption that some former profession insures God's acceptance is presumptuous at best, and sheer folly at worst, because there is no humanly discernable guarantee of perseverance for those who demonstrate so little love for God. People cannot know they "are called according to his [God's] purpose" (v. 28) if they are not living in accord with God's purposes. Individuals cannot claim the promise of perseverance if there is no evidence they love God.

Thus, the promise of perseverance forces us always to examine whether our lives conform to God's expectations and standards. Does what we do show love for him and faithfulness to the purpose for which we are called? We answer by asking ourselves familiar questions. Is there any evidence that my love for God is real? Do my attitudes and actions reveal a living, vibrant love for God and his purposes? There can be no "dead" orthodoxy among us if the promise of perseverance persists in our minds and governs our actions. We will examine both what we *believe* and what we *do* in our daily lives and we will ask, "Does what I am doing reflect love for my God?" Our work habits, our entertainments, and our relationships will all be measured against this fundamental standard that involves our hearts in holiness far more than slavish obedience to artificial systems of human do's and don'ts that dishearten many believers and exasperate others. Religion stops being a game of moral chess played against God where we are always questioning, "Why don't I have a right to do this? Can anyone prove me wrong? Or, where in the Bible does it say I cannot . . . ?" Such questions create a legal-loophole spirituality in which we approach God as a threatening antagonist whom we must outsmart at his own religious game. Perseverance allows Christians to consider God and his purposes far more positively.

Minds and hearts that properly apprehend the wonderful promise of perseverance ask questions that reflect their security and God's love. Because the perseverance of grace assures us of God's eternal desire to hold us, we are freed from the futility of trying to match wits with him. We are able to search his Word for what he requires with the confidence that he desires only what is good for us. Because we know he wants our hearts to be bound to his own, we are able to ask ourselves, "Does what I am doing express love for my God who sacrificed his Son for me?" Such questions are far less concerned with self than they are with the honor, the glory, and the name of our Lord. The promise of perseverance allows us to concentrate on the questions that result in true holiness, because we can be more concerned about whether our actions reflect love for God than whether we can avoid his rejection. When perseverance is understood, loving service replaces begrudging obedience or legalistic righteousness. The promise of perseverance substitutes concern for self-preservation with love for God's purposes.

Prompts Love

The promise of persevering grace not only conforms our actions to God's standards by allowing us to focus on our love for him, but perseverance also prompts our love for each other. If we truly love God, then our hearts desire what pleases him. We love what he loves. This means *those* God loves we must also love. None of us can honestly say we love God whom we have not seen and then not love fellow Christians (who are created in the image of God) whom we have seen (1 John 4:20). The same perseverance promise that causes us to examine whether our actions express love for God forces us to examine whether our attitudes reflect love for others. Hearts as well as actions must be in accord with God's purposes if we are to have any assurance that we will persevere in God's grace.

Attitude Checks

The conclusion that our attitudes toward others are as much a confirmation of our relationship with God as our personal actions may trouble some believers. Every religious movement and faith tradition has its weaknesses. As I look back over my ministry to view my attitudes and the ones I was taught, I am convinced that one of our greatest strengths is one of our greatest weaknesses. In our circles we do not just study doctrine, we are committed to it. We are a cerebral bunch. So committed are we to the truths we believe the Bible teaches that our tendency is first to slight those who disagree with us. Then, if they do not accept our correction, we tend to accuse, to ridicule, or to condemn. Often we end up turning on each other because even we do not see everything eye to eye.

Perhaps I am talking more about myself than others, but I recognize my early years of ministry to be characterized by arrogance, pride of knowledge, pride of distinctives, intolerance of differences, and disrespect of others not of my persuasion. I desire only that others not follow my errant path. By saying this I do not ask that any abandon their doctrinal commitments, but I implore each person to understand that doctrinal commitment without compassion is heresy. Orthodoxy with arrogance is falsehood. Slander for the sake of truth is a lie. Disrespect for those whose genuine convictions differ is not godly. Love of God without love for other Christians is not really love for God.

We must be cautious of men and movements whose commitment to orthodoxy is couched in expressions of hatred, suspicion, and anger—not necessarily because their doctrine is wrong, but because their love for God is misguided. Some causes are worth fighting for, but not at the expense of our own holiness. Whether or not we agree with persons whose opinions differ from ours, God requires that we act lovingly toward those he loves. Love for others does not mean we will fail to differ with them or that we may not strive for what we believe is right. But disagreement does not require disrespect. Striving for our convictions does not necessitate abandonment of our commitment to godly attitudes. The orthodoxy of our beliefs does not relieve us from the obligations of faith. All things work together for good only for those who love God. Assurance of our own eternal security requires we love him enough to love those he loves.

Empty Hands

Perseverance not only conforms our actions to God's standards, it also conforms our hearts to his will. The sanctifying power of perseverance results from the careful scrutiny it requires we give both our personal actions and attitudes toward others. Inevitably this examination exposes the inadequacy of our actions and attitudes to bind us to God. No one acts as righteously as God requires or loves as fully as he desires. He must hold us, because our weaknesses declare our inadequacy of holding to him. If perseverance is untrue—if we really must maintain our relationship with God—then we are all destined for hell. Our best works are too interwoven with threads of human motives and strands of human frailty to bind us to God. If he holds us not, then we are not held at all. But since he holds us, nothing can take us from him (Rom. 8:38–39).

God's promise of perseverance instills deep love and total humility in our hearts. Our love for him deepens because we perceive how gracious he is. Our humility deepens because we understand how dependent we are on his provision. Because our eternal security is totally dependent on him, we can exhibit no pride or boasting or self-claim of any sort. We are secure only because of him. We can look down on no one. No works from us or attitudes in us gain God's affection. Our best works are still filthy rags. When we have done all we can do, we are still unworthy servants (see Luke 17:10). That is why an honest appraisal of our ability to meet God's holy standards always leads us to Christ (see Gal. 3:24). All is grace. All we are, all we can be, all this world shall be, is of grace. No law or set of standards or system will ever usher us into the kingdom. We must remember our dependence lest we become theocentric (believing we are holy because we think and talk about godly things) rather than Christo-centric. Holiness is from God, through Christ Jesus and through no other source. If the cross becomes background to any movement, it is not of God, though it speaks of him often. We do not achieve holiness; Christ grants it. We do not win grace; Jesus provides it. We do not secure ourselves to heaven; God holds us to himself by means of the cross alone.

The provision of perseverance reminds us of Francis Schaeffer's "empty hands of faith." We must come to God claiming no goodness or ability in ourselves. We must reach for him with our hands emptied of all our own accomplishments or craft. We must approach him recognizing our total dependence on him. In doing so, our hearts are made humble, thankful, and ever-appreciative of the cross. Our holiness becomes an expression of gratitude for what God has done in our behalf, rather than selfish striving for what he can do in our behalf. In this change of heart resides our fullest assurance of eternal security. Just as a heart turned from hostility toward God is evidence of the working of the Holy Spirit (Rom. 8:6–8), so a heart tuned to humble love for God is the mark of God's hold on us.

Resonating Hearts

The Jefferson Barracks Bridge, which crosses the Mississippi River near St. Louis, reflects an architectural design called the tied arch. A series of cables suspend the roadbed from one massive supporting arch. For the bridge to support the intended load, the cables must be at a very specific tension. It is not enough that the cables look as though they can support the weight, or even that they partially do the job for which they were intended. If the tension is improper, the whole support system is jeopardized. To adjust the cables and insure the integrity of the bridge, a sensing device is placed on the cables. It tests tension by plucking each cable like a huge harp string to see if it is tuned to the proper resonance. Whether the bridge will hold is revealed by the tone each cable emits. In a similar way God's hold on us is revealed by the tone of our hearts.

When our hearts resonate with love for God, we can be assured that our relationship with him is secure. If we are looking at outward signs of performance, we will have no real assurance of heaven's support. Appearances are too deceiving. People can make terrible mistakes by evaluating their own spiritual security or that of others based on outward conformity to God's standards. It is certainly true that if we have no intention of carrying out heaven's requirements, there is no assurance the bridge between heaven and our hearts will hold. However, honest assessment of any life reveals no one does all heaven requires. That is why it is necessary to pluck our own heart strings in prayer and honest reflection to test whether our hearts resonate with God's heart. The tone that is truly Christian reverberates with loving humility for the forgiveness our sin requires and echoes grateful obedience for the grace our God provides. The promises of perseverance require us to test whether these attitudes resonate in our hearts, because there alone can we discover the integrity of our relationship with God. Even when the tone emitted is not yet as strong as we might wish (and may take some additional adjustment), yet when our hearts beat in tune with God's heart, the bridge between heaven and us is secure.

The former pastor's wife, whose story I told in the last chapter, in evaluating the integrity of her relationship with God, made the mistake of measuring her own assurance by the commitment of another's heart. Certainly it was true her pastor husband had exhibited many outward signs of his salvation. It is possible that he is still a Christian in terrible rebellion. But in the light of his continuing adultery, there can be no assurance that he has, or had, any real relationship with God. Only God knows if this pastor is still held by the grace of God or never actually experienced saving grace. In every church Christians grieve that there are those who turn their backs on what seemed to be a once vital faith. But people should not evaluate the integrity of their own faith on the basis of others' actions. We may believe we see evidence of another's saved heart, but ultimately only they have the potential for sure insight into their own hearts. Christians should never evaluate God's hold on them by another's failure. In their hearts is the answer as to whether they are secure in God's care. They must carefully look in God's Word and inside their own hearts to discern the perseverance God promises.

Provides Confidence

Because the power of God holds Christians who desire to fulfill his purposes, they are marvelously equipped to serve him. They can attempt great things for God without the fear that their failure will mean they have fallen from his grace. Their confidence of his care enables them to stride into great personal danger without fear of spiritual harm and to move forward boldly.

An automobile commercial a few years ago pictured a beautifully dressed young woman with an expensive car perched atop a towering rock pinnacle in a western desert. Each side of the narrow pinnacle was a sheer cliff hundreds of feet high. A misstep in any direction would mean certain death. The commercial was meant to emphasize the wonder of the car's styling and performance, but I suspect that viewers thought much more about how scared the young model must have been and about how much the company must have paid her to pose in such danger.

Paralyzing fear would grip anyone of sound mind who is in danger of walking off a cliff in any direction. Prudence would dictate that to keep from falling from safety, one should not take even the smallest step. If our holiness is only a precarious, dizzying height from which we may fall because we are blind to where future steps may lead, then prudence would dictate that we must not make the slightest move. Better to stand still than take the smallest step that might send us over the cliff on which our salvation is perched. But God has no desire for us to be paralyzed. He has great and mighty purposes for us to pursue. That is why he provides the perseverance promises that assure us we are not standing on a pinnacle of salvation. We stand on the vast plain of God's mercy. The victimized, former pastor's wife who hesitated to move forward with her life because she worried she might blindly run off the cliff of her salvation can set aside her fear.

We are not blind and we are not on a cliff. By God's grace we see an expanse of mercy that extends to the farthest horizon of our lives. Thus, we can move forward in the tasks he sets before us with strength, energy, and courage; not because the path is easy but because the way is sure. What path can scare us if God himself prepares the way? What purpose can intimidate us if he promises his provision to the end?

The confidence that sure provision provides was well demonstrated by a couple my family knows. The young couple struggled to make ends meet while attending seminary. Earning enough even to purchase food was a problem. At the beginning of each month they worried whether they would be eating in the final week. The worrying was almost worse than the lack of money. If one of them got sick early in the month, they would not go to the doctor lest the medical bill deny them food money. The couple would never go out for fun or even a birthday dinner because other expenses might occur later in the month. Their lives were controlled by the fear of what might happen later each month. Then they hit on a clever solution that gave them courage, confidence, and great release. They went out early one month, while there was still money in the budget, and bought thirty large cans of pork and beans. They lined the cans up on the pantry shelf, one for each day of the month, and stopped worrying. Now no matter what happened they knew they would not starve that month. They would persevere. There were enough beans to keep them going to the end of the month even if they spent their remaining money on other things.

By filling their pantry with pork and beans the couple made sure they had a month's supply of canned meals. As a result of this simple provision, their lives changed. The paralyzing fear of tomorrow that previously kept the couple from making prudent or pleasant choices vanished from their lives. The assurance of sufficiency to reach each month's end gave them freedom to do what each month required. Finances were still tight, but the young couple was no longer crippled by fret. They would make it! Confidence gave them new vitality for life and fresh release from anxiety. They could face each day with courage because they saw their future was secure.

God grants us similar confidence, not necessarily with thirty cans of beans, but with the promise of persevering grace. He shows us a secure future by telling us he is working all things together for good. We are released from paralysis because we know we are called for a purpose. The promises may seem distant at times. When we are struggling at school, when we are isolated from the support of other Christians where we work, or when it seems that we shall never see the fruit of our labors, we can begin to doubt if there is purpose in what we are doing. We may wonder if our service is all for nothing, or if anything good can possibly come out of our feeble efforts, frequent mistakes, and impossible situations. In these times we must remember the God who holds us securely and will carry us through until the end of his purposes. The God who says he will bring to completion the good work he begins in us will not let us down (see Phil. 1:6).

The Father's Grasp

My wife's favorite verse from the nativity narratives is "Mary treasured up all these things and pondered them in her heart" (Luke 2:19). The prescient events of Christ's birth were precious reminders of God's promises throughout the life of Mary's Son. As she looked at her infant she remembered the work of salvation promised through her child. When he sat among the wood shavings in the carpenter's shop as a toddler, she heard the echo of the angels' praise. When his teenage jaw began to show the strength of maturity, she reflected on the honor shepherds had given him. How important her treasured thoughts must have been when her husband was gone and her Son was an outcast. Did she remember the songs of the angels when men spat upon her Son and put the nails in his hands? Could a mother have avoided asking, "When, O God, when will you honor the treasures of my heart? Lord, is there any purpose in what I have pondered?" We know the answers to Mary's likely questions. God accomplished his good as he said he would. The implausible fulfillment of seemingly impossible promises was secure because God's purposes are incontrovertible.

God's commitment to fulfill his promises in the face of great challenges to his purposes is a treasure for us to ponder still. We can trust him to secure our salvation despite spiritual trials, because he has promised to secure our futures and has proven himself faithful in the past. Even when we have questions about what God is doing, we have the promise of divine purpose in his Word, the proof of infinite love at the cross, and the proclamation of persevering grace for our hearts.

These assurances of God's faithfulness grant us the confidence that makes our lives joyful in the face of spiritual adversity. God will persevere in completing his plans. Since he has called us for his purpose, he will preserve us for that good end. God's ultimate good may not be achieved at the end of easy roads and pleasant circumstances, but the promise that our heavenly Father will hold us in his care reassures us for the tasks that are ahead.

The joy that a father's grasp can bestow is especially evident during the Christmas season in our home. We prepare for the day of Christ's birth by reading portions of the Advent narratives each night for the two weeks before Christmas. We use a manger scene to recreate the events that we read to the children. Each night after we finish the reading, we add the nativity figures to the manger scene that reflect the portion of the story we have just read. Actually, we parents do not put the shepherds and sheep, wise men and camels in place. Our children have the privilege of placing the large ceramic figures on the mantel. The task is not easy for them. Being small, our children can hardly reach the mantel, much less place the large, heavy figurines. Yet, though the task is impossible for them, they can hardly wait to do it every year.

The reason our children look forward to an impossible task is that they know it does not depend on their ability. The results are sure, because although they cannot reach the mantel and though the ceramic figures are in constant danger of breaking while in their little hands, they are confident of other hands to help them. Despite their inadequacies they bubble with joy, because they trust my grasp. I pick them up and lift them higher than they can reach so that they can accomplish their purpose. Because their father holds them, our children complete the story of Jesus in our home each year.

We believers cannot know all that awaits us, but we do know that our Father promises to hold us. The heights of holiness we cannot reach do not cause us to despair, because he lifts us up and will never let us fall. We can move forward in our tasks with courage, confidence, and great anticipation because of the Father who holds us to complete the story of Jesus in our hearts forever.

QUESTIONS *for Thought*

1. Why is the phrase "once saved, always saved" a poor representation of the Bible's teaching on perseverance?
2. How does the promise of persevering grace promote holiness?

3. What is the sure destiny of every one of us if our actions or attitudes are what maintain our relationship with God? Why?
4. How does God's hold on us better equip us to serve him?

PART FOUR

Jesus' Love

NINE

The Best Promise

W hat is your favorite ice-cream sundae topping? For some it's nuts. Others most enjoy the whipped cream, chocolate syrup, caramel coating, or shredded coconut. But for me there is no question which topping is the best. The part of any sundae that I love most is the cherry on top. That which is put on last is stacked on top for a very good reason as I see it: The best bite gets the most privileged position.

Perhaps a similar reasoning possessed the Westminster authors when they decided where to put this final promise of God in their list of promises that apply to all Christians. The promise that dominates the latter portions of this chapter of Romans is the *assurance of God's love*. This promise actually occurs first on the Westminster Catechism list of God's promises:

> The benefits which in this life accompany or flow from justification, adoption and sanctification include:
> assurance of God's love,
> peace of conscience,
> joy in the Holy Ghost,
> increase of grace,
> and perseverance therein to the end.

I am sure there is a sophisticated theological argument for the order of these promises. But for me no exhaustive explanation is needed. The reason the authors stacked this last promise first on their list is obvious. It's the cherry on top!

Romans 8:31–39

[31]What, then, shall we say in response to this? If God is for us, who can be against us? [32]He who did not spare his own Son, but gave him up for us all—how will he not also, along with him, graciously give us all things? [33]Who will bring any charge against those whom God has chosen? It is God who justifies. [34]Who is he that condemns? Christ Jesus, who died—more than that, who was raised to life—is at the right hand of God and is also interceding for us. [35]Who shall separate us from the love of Christ? Shall trouble or hardship or persecution or famine or nakedness or danger or sword? [36]As it is written:

> "For your sake we face death all day long;
> we are considered as sheep to be slaughtered."

[37]No, in all these things we are more than conquerors through him who loved us. [38]For I am convinced that neither death nor life, neither angels nor demons, neither the present nor the future, nor any powers, [39]neither height

nor depth, nor anything else in all creation, will be able to separate us from the love of God that is in Christ Jesus our Lord.

Your First Theology Lesson

Do you remember your first theology lesson? Do not believe that because you have not been to Bible college or seminary that you have not studied theology. Anytime you learn something about God you have a theology lesson. I even know what your first theology lesson is likely to have been. There is really no mystery about how I know. The lesson many of us learned first is still taught all over the world in hundreds of different languages. For countless millions of Christians it goes like this:

> Jesus loves me, this I know,
> For the Bible tells me so;
> Little ones to him belong,
> They are weak, but he is strong.
> Yes, Jesus loves me! Yes, Jesus loves me!
> Yes, Jesus loves me! The Bible tells me so.

Why was this the first song so many of us were taught? Because it is simple? Surely, that is part of the answer. But I suspect there is more cause than simplicity alone.

We teach the song of Jesus' love to young children because its promises are so important to us. The understanding that Jesus loves me is the core of what each Christian must believe. We teach this truth early in our children's lives because we know the reality of Christ's love must be planted deep into the very fiber of each maturing believer. Young hearts and minds must learn to grasp this elemental promise in the earliest moments of faith, because so much of what awaits them in life will threaten to rob them of the assurance of God's love. Personal sin, difficult circumstances, and the spiritual forces of Satan unite to war against the assurance of Jesus' love in all believers' hearts in all ages.

We are certain the assurance of Jesus' love will be challenged and can be shaken. The reason we are so certain is that our own assurance of Christ's love is challenged daily, and some of us have been shaken. Some now reading this book may doubt Jesus' love. Since first making a faith commitment, the ecstasy of your early experience in Christ may have waned. You may be less changed than you believe God can accept. The Christian life may be more difficult than you anticipated. People you trusted may be less holy than you expected. In the midst of these observations you may wonder if God's love is real. Even if you are not asking similar questions now, remember that all Christians are susceptible to such doubt. You do something, or something painful happens, and a voice in you whispers, "Does Jesus really love me?" It is not a question of which you need to be ashamed.

God knows our assurance of his love can be shaken. So even in this most sophisticated of New Testament books, where the apostle Paul is weaving theological arguments and historical facts from all of Scripture, God has him return to this simple theme at the center of the epistle. You can almost hear God whisper to the apostle, saying, "Now, Paul, this is rather difficult for my people to understand and there is more they need to know. So, lest they get discouraged, let's remind them one more time Jesus loves them, and nothing can change that." Accordingly, at the heart of his letter, Paul writes that nothing can separate true believers from the love of God that is in Christ Jesus—not sin, nor circumstances, nor spiritual opposition. Whatever is going on in your life, whatever has happened, whatever will occur, Paul says this assurance is yours to claim as a believer:

> Jesus loves me, this I know,
> For the Bible tells me so.

Love Greater than Sin

Paul assures us of the comprehensive promise of God's love by first addressing doubts that originate inside of us. Guilt over personal sin can shake our confidence that God loves us. So Paul begins by saying we must believe the love of Jesus is greater than all our sin.

Paul reminds believers that our sin does not set God against us. God is now *for* us, because he did not spare his own Son but gave Jesus as a sacrifice to suffer for our sins (vv. 31–32). The penalty for sin that we deserve, God put on his own Son. When we confess our sin, we bear its guilt no longer. Our sin cannot separate us from God, because God takes the guilt away. We are assured of the love of God despite our sin, because in Christ's sacrifice God shows that his love overcomes our sin. The cross shows how much he loves us and how he can keep loving us. Because Christ's sacrifice purchased God's pardon, personal sin does not deny us God's love. Having drawn that sword of truth, Paul now cuts two directions against the internal threats to our faith that originate in conscience. The apostle attacks the challenges of past sin and present sin, which war against our assurance of God's love through human guilt.

Love Greater than Past Sin

With an emphasis that seems almost harsh, Paul continues to drive home the point that our sin does not deny us God's acceptance. The apostle asks who can condemn us if God has justified us by setting aside the charges against us (v. 33). Paul's argument reflects a legal standard we yet recognize. If the highest judge of the land has already pardoned someone for a past crime, then that person cannot again be charged for the wrong. If the highest judge of the universe has pardoned your sin, then your conscience should not condemn you. It is actually incredibly presumptuous to ignore the pardon of divine justice and assume guilt even if that guilt comes from our own hearts. Paul speaks this forcefully because he knows our hearts often echo guilt more loudly than grace.

Our past sins haunt us. Guilt for past wrongs may grab us so quickly and may strike so unexpectedly that its assault may surprise even the most seasoned believer. We may be going about some daily routine, and suddenly an ad in a newspaper or a song on the radio reminds us of something in the past, and an old guilt grabs us again. Perhaps we see a look in our own child's eyes that brings us face-to-face with ourselves; a sin we thought was dead years ago suddenly stares out at us in the look of a little one who reflects what we do not want to see in ourselves. Though we have confessed that sin and prayed for God's forgiveness, somehow now repentance does not seem enough. The reminder makes the guilt fresh. Trials we experience right now may seem to witness against us, proving we are guilty again, dirty again, and unlikely to be children of God.

Intervening years are no guarantee our hearts will not resurrect a dead guilt. I have preached in many churches where hearts have made past sin come to life again. I have preached on abortion and witnessed hearts torn as both women and men faced their participation in the horror. I have preached on immorality and watched silent tears confess a hidden past. I have preached on Christian family principles and seen parents' heads drop in shame while sitting next to wayward children. I do not regret the words that convict of sin. There is no more rewarding time in ministry than when God's people see their sin and seek him. I rejoice to see God heal broken hearts with the truths of his Word. But I cease to rejoice when my words cause God's forgiveness to be doubted or re-create guilt for sin that has long since been confessed.

A few years ago I preached a sermon on God's judgment of adultery. After the message a distraught young woman approached me. With many tears and obvious heartache, she said she was guilty of such sin. She told what she had done and then asked, "How can I ever get rid of this guilt?" I encouraged her to confess the matter fully to the Lord and ask his forgiveness. When she responded, it was my turn to weep. She said, "Oh, I did that five years ago."

I wondered what I had said or done that made this young woman think that God's pardon was not enough. I wanted to hold her and ask her forgiveness saying, "What did you hear me say that made you think that once you have properly repented of sin that God still wants you to feel this guilt?" I recognize that as a minister of the gospel of Jesus Christ it is my duty to seek to convict of sin, but that is never my end goal. My task as a servant of Jesus is not merely to convict of sin but to convince of grace. Pastors may learn to love the tears of guilt more than the tears of joy, because the former are often easier to elicit. But a minister's longing for affirmation of effectiveness never warrants the withholding of God's promise of complete pardon for sincere repentance. Our constant message for God's people must be, "Gather all the guilt that is yours— nothing more and nothing less—take it to the cross of Jesus and lay it down. Then do not pick it up again. It is not yours anymore."

Of course, people may experience continuing guilt for incomplete repentance. The human heart is complex enough that serious sin may require more than formula prayers and simple maxims before full forgiveness is felt or warranted. Sin can twist itself into the deepest recesses of the human conscience where it cannot be purged by a person merely mouthing words of contrition. Repentance that leads to grace requires us to bare our souls before God's holy love with honest sorrow and the humble desire that God's Spirit would reveal and forgive any further darkness to which our sinful consciences are blind. Such sincere repentance may require much soul searching and personal reflection. For this reason we should examine ourselves for dimensions of sin we've not previously recognized so that we can fully know the joy of forgiveness. But no human heart is so discerning of the depth of its own sin and the righteousness of God that the promise of full forgiveness should be made contingent upon human perceptions. We are forgiven because of our plea for grace and our acknowledgement that we can never fathom the depth of our need, not because we have completely identified the sin that God alone can fully see.

God's grace does not depend on our inadequate capabilities to comprehend fully the depth of our sins. While we more fully appreciate and experience grace to the extent that we understand our need of it, we should not portray God's forgiveness as relying upon the degree of guilt we can make ourselves feel. The goal of pastors and of all caring believers must be to lead others out of guilt, not into guilt. Just as it is never right to convince a Christian that God's pardon for what was truly confessed is questionable, it is detrimental to the gospel to gear a ministry toward making Christians perpetually wonder if they have repented enough or felt enough shame to gain God's pardon.

Christ did not die so that we would be more burdened. The faithlessness that burdens all prior to conversion results from failure to believe in Christ's pardon. But the faithfulness that still burdens many Christians results from the failure to receive Christ's pardon. There is no benefit and no merit in denying the effectiveness of Christ's sacrifice for our sin. God's desire is that we would be free of the weight of our sin so that we can be released to serve him fully. Christians should rejoice in the forgiveness that frees from guilt, not wallow in the guilt that they hope will purchase forgiveness. Only the blood of Christ purchases our pardon, and that purchase has already been made. If God, as the highest judge, says our worst sins are forgiven because of the work of his Son, then we have no right to condemn ourselves. Rather, we have the privilege of confessing past sin and the responsibility of expressing present joy for the pardon he has already purchased.

We should take no pleasure in seeing any Christian grieve for what God has declared past and gone. We should long to see the tears of joy that say, "Yes, I did sin. It's all true. I was guilty. But, praise God, I am free of that. God gave his Son to release me from my guilt. My sins are covered by Christ's sacrifice. What is past is passed over by God's grace. Jesus loves me despite my past. The Bible tells me so."

Love Greater than Present Sin

But what if the sin is not past? What if, though we believe God forgives past sin, today's sin eats at our hearts and consciences? Christians often discover it is far easier to appreciate God's pardoning the wrong they did when they knew no better, than to experience forgiveness of their present sin when they now know very well what God requires. Tempers, temptations, and our tongues can rule us despite past confessions. Current fault makes us feel worthless not only because we know better but often because we recognize this is not the first time we have been weak in this way. We hate the sin that characterizes our lives and wonder if a holy God feels the same about us.

By causing us to question our relationship with God, present guilt may actually propel Christians into deeper sin. Doubts of God's continuing care make it easy to think, "What's the use of trying to stop? God doesn't love me anyway. Since I'm already lost, why fight it?" Paul battles such resignation that would lead to greater sin by assuring us that God's love covers wrong that we commit today as well as yesterday. The apostle reminds us that Christ's past acts of death and resurrection are not the end of his work in our behalf. Paul says Jesus intercedes for us at God's right hand *now* (v. 34). The apostle uses the present tense of the Greek word, denoting action that continues to express this work of Christ. Jesus never stops interceding for us. There is only one reason Jesus would stay at God's right hand to keep asking for our forgiveness today: He knows we need forgiveness today. Jesus intercedes in the present tense because we sin in the present tense. Christ's presence at God's right hand assures us that even present sin will not deny us God's love. Our actions may grieve God and hurt us, but they can never rob us of his love, because Christ does not stop interceding for us. Nothing can separate us from the love of God when God's own Son intercedes for us.

Christ's continual intercession insures the constancy of God's love. Guilt makes this constancy difficult to grasp, but the truth must be held firmly by every Christian or despair is sure to result. Alexander Whyte, minister and scholar in the Free Church of Scotland almost a century ago, illustrated how necessary it is to remember the constancy of God's mercy by telling of the spiritual devastation that nearly devoured an older saint who forgot. Whyte told of working late into the evening on various matters of church business with an older minister of the church. Their business was complex and tiring, yet when the matters were resolved the older minister lingered even later in idle conversation. He seemed to want to say something but was never quite able to get to the point. Finally, in what sounded almost like a jest, the man said to Dr. Whyte, "Now, sir, have you any word of comfort for an old sinner like me?"

Somehow, beneath the pasted-on smile, Dr. Whyte saw the question was one of real seriousness and deep agony. He wrote later, "It took my breath away. He was an old saint. But he did not know the peace of forgiveness." Not knowing what best to do, Dr. Whyte simply rose from his chair, took the hand of the older minister and said, "He delights in showing mercy," words from the prophet Micah expressing God's constant love (Mic. 7:18).

Not much more was said by either man. The two parted for the evening. The next morning a letter came to Dr. Whyte from the older minister. It read: "Dear friend, I will never doubt Him again. Guilt had hold of me. I was near the gates of Hell, but that word of God comforted me, and I will never doubt Him again. I will never despair again. If the devil casts my sin in my teeth, I will say, 'Yes, it is all true, and you cannot tell the half of it, but I have to deal with the One who delights in showing mercy.'"

The Key of Mercy

The Lord does not just forgive. He delights to do so. It brings God joy to show mercy, because by forgiving us he answers the intercessions of his own Son who speaks in our behalf. Therefore, if our minds and hearts continue to condemn us after genuine confession, we should realize that condemnation is not of God. God sent his Son to die for our sin, not to keep our guilt alive. In the light of Christ's sacrifice for our sin the apostle asks, "Who is he that condemns?" (Rom. 8:34). Believers know the answer. The Bible says that Satan is the accuser of God's children (Rev. 12:10). He is the one who whispers in our consciences that our sin is so terrible, Jesus cannot love us now. Satan is the one who brings our guilt to mind again and again to burden us so we cannot serve God effectively.

God wants us to remember his mercy whenever we consider our sin. My wife says she sometimes pictures in her mind a locked file cabinet that holds all her past sins that Jesus has put away. Occasionally there is another sin to add to the files, but she says that in her mind she will open that file only with a key labeled mercy. Even though Satan sometimes tempts her to rifle through those files of memory, she has resolved never to open any drawer to the past or file away any sin in the present unless mercy opens the cabinet. The God who delights in mercy invites all of us to do the same.

Satan parades the sin in your mind to rob your heart of the assurance of God's love and to sap your life of the strength that comes from knowing God will not reject you. Do not stand for it! Jesus died to pay the price for your sin. He rose to defeat the power of sin over you. Now he intercedes for you at the right hand of God to make sure that God's care will never fail you. So when Satan creeps into your conscience to condemn you, look to the cross where your sins were cancelled and say to him, "Yes, it's all true, and you know not the half of it, but I have to deal with the One who delights in showing mercy. Jesus loves me. This I know, for the Bible tells me so."

QUESTIONS *for Thought*

1. Why does God speak with such repetition and force about his justification in this portion of Romans 8?

2. Who condemns sinners when God has justified them? How does this condemnation occur?
3. Does the extent of God's grace depend upon the degree of guilt we feel? Why?
4. How do we know that God provides grace for present as well as past sin?
5. How should God's provision of grace affect the way we consider our sin?

TEN

The Greatest Love

Love Greater than Circumstances

The guilt that causes Christians to question God's love is a consequence of internal thoughts and emotions. But our assurance of God's love can also be shaken by external factors. Difficult circumstances can cause us to question if Jesus loves us. We wonder if what we are going through indicates that God has rejected or forgotten us. Paul reassures us that hardship is no barometer of the love of God: "Who shall separate us from the love of Christ? Shall trouble or hardship or persecution or famine or nakedness or danger or sword? No, in all these things we are more than conquerors through him who loved us" (Rom. 8:35–37). Circumstances may press us, but they do not separate us from the love of God. God's care prevails even when troubles come.

Some time ago friends of ours thought their new baby was arriving earlier than expected. Because the trip to the hospital was off the anticipated schedule, plans they had made for others to watch their two-year-old son during delivery fell through. As a result we received a desperate telephone call, "Can you watch little Stevie? The new baby is coming and we have to get to the hospital."

We said sure we would watch the two-year-old, and in a few minutes a harried father dropped little Stevie off at our door. All went fine until bedtime. Little Stevie was not thrilled about going to bed in a strange house without his mom and dad. To make matters worse a thunderstorm started to rumble over the house just as we slipped Stevie into his pajamas. We put him in bed, and I began to pat his back to try to calm him. My arm wore out long before Stevie nodded off. Then, just as his eyelids seemed ready to close for the last time, our doorbell rang.

Standing at our door in the pouring rain was Stevie's father. With a sheepish grin he said, "Sorry, false alarm." Stevie's new little brother or sister was not going to arrive that night. The soaking wet, slightly embarrassed father came inside to retrieve the two-year-old who was supposed to be sleeping. But as we walked down the hallway toward Stevie's bedroom door a huge thunderclap suddenly shook the house. The windows were still rattling when Stevie, in the form of a white-cotton-pajama streak, flew out of the bedroom. He bolted down the hall and ran right into his father's arms. The father held his child close and said, "It's all right, Stevie. I'm here." Then, though the storm still blew and the thunder still roared, the child did not cry anymore because he knew he was in his father's care.

Though storms may still enter our lives and though difficulties may yet thunder about us, we do not despair because we are in our Father's care. Christ removed the barrier of sin, and now nothing can separate us from the loving arms of our heavenly Father. This does not mean the Christian life is without pain. Paul readily concedes that believers will face sufferings and persecutions in this world (v. 36). But Paul victoriously concludes that such things cannot overcome God's love (v. 37). Even when our world terrifies us, our God holds us close to himself through the work of Jesus. In that embrace of grace our worst fears are conquered. We realize that circumstances do not deny his care, because our heavenly Father keeps whispering in his Word, "I'm right here, child. I'm right here. You are in my care."

Because affirmations of God's care may only echo faintly when difficulties thunder, Paul makes sure his readers hear the promise of God's continuing love. The apostle reiterates the truth three times in this passage. Earlier in the chapter Paul tells us that our present sufferings are not worth comparing with the glory that we will know when Christ returns (v. 18). The words remind us that if God loved us enough to sacrifice his Son to save us in the past, and if we will experience the riches of his love in the future, then God must also love us in the time between, even if it holds some difficulty. Through his apostle God says to each of us, "If I love you at the beginning of our journey and promise to love you when we reach our destination, then there is no reason to doubt my love along the way, even if the road gets bumpy."

As further confirmation of God's unwavering love, Paul tells us that God works all things together for our good (v. 28). The afflictions we experience do not evidence the absence of divine love, because God uses even this pain for higher purposes in our behalf. The proof is in the cross itself. In Christ's sacrifice God was at work doing his good when only evil was immediately apparent. Still, it can strain credulity to believe there could be any purpose in the suffering and horror that we must occasionally face in this fallen world. Without a divine perspective the world often appears senseless and without confirmation of God's continuing love. For this reason, Paul's most compelling proof that difficult circumstances do not prove the absence of divine love is saved for last.

The ultimate reason we know that difficult circumstances do not indicate loss of our value to God is that he already purchased us at too high a price not to consider us precious to himself now (v. 32). We are so valuable to God that he purchased our souls at the cost of his own Son's blood. Since he purchased us at such an infinite price, it would be preposterous now, simply because we face some difficulty, to assume that we are not of tremendous value to God.

I have learned from my wife that difficult circumstances do not cancel personal value. Kathy is a gifted musician. When I first began dating her, I had to learn a few things about the special relationship between a professional musician and her instrument. I once picked her up after a concert and started to put her flute in the trunk of my car along with our coats and a music stand. I quickly learned that the flute would not go in the trunk. That flute would not even ride in the back seat of the car. It had to ride in the front seat with us.

Kathy cared so much for that flute because she spent years working and saving to buy the quality instrument. Since that date early in our relationship, I have seen my wife play her instrument in a great variety of circumstances. I have seen her play under hot lights, in freezing cold, even in driving rain. But no matter how difficult the circumstances in which she uses her flute, I never doubt its value to her. She sacrificed too much for the instrument for me ever to doubt its preciousness to her.

For the same reason we believers must never doubt our preciousness to God. God may need to use us in difficult circumstances, but he sacrificed too much for us not to care about us now. God may need to use us as an instrument of salvation in a difficult marriage. He may need our testimony in a time of illness or financial pressure. But none of these hardships indicate we are not precious to God. He purchased us at too high a price for us ever to need to question our value to him.

Circumstances cannot deny the care of the one who gave his life for me. Despite my trials, this I know: Jesus loves me; the Bible tells me so.

Love Greater than Satan

Beyond each of us are more than circumstances that may drive a wedge between us and our assurance of God's love. As much a reality for the apostle Paul as the challenges of the physical world are the spiritual forces around us that war against our faith. When he lists all the forces of this world that cannot separate us from the love of God, Paul includes angels, demons, powers, heights, and depths (vv. 38–39). The words echo other reminders from Paul that believers are involved daily in spiritual warfare. "We wrestle not against flesh and blood, but against principalities and powers, against the rulers of darkness of this world, against spiritual forces of evil in high places" (Eph. 6:12). We live in a world where we have spiritual foes who are seeking to destroy our confidence in God.

Because Paul knows the forces of evil are real, he takes great care to assure us the love of Jesus is always greater than Satan's assaults. The apostle actually reserves his most eloquent and most vigorous assurances for this portion of his message because he knows how easily we may discount what is often the greatest threat to our faith. In our culture, concepts of spiritual evil too easily degenerate into Halloween images of little urchins with pointed tails or the special effects in the latest horror movie. Such images blind us to the reality that Paul sees.

I do not believe I have seen the forces of evil more vividly than during my last year of seminary. The school I attended had a tradition of letting every senior preach in chapel before the entire student body and faculty. These senior sermons were supposed to be the crowning achievements of our seminary experience as we exhibited all we had learned. What I needed to learn did not occur to me until I was almost done preaching my sermon. For my text I chose Matthew 6:25–34, which speaks of our heavenly Father's abiding care. The words came easily until I realized the faith it took to receive them. As I looked out over my classmates, I noticed that I did not have a single close friend who had not faced a major life crisis during his years in seminary. That reality hit me like an electric jolt. I thought, "Someone doesn't want us here. Someone doesn't want us to go from this place to share the gospel. There seems to be an undeniable pattern of attack on the people who are here to drive them away from the purposes for which they came." Suddenly I realized I had been blind to the spiritual warfare that had been going on all about me.

Satan's forces are real and active. Evil is not fiction. We are terribly vulnerable to spiritual oppression and depression if we do not recognize the real potential of spiritual attack. Such attacks are not confined to seminary communities. Every one of us believers is considered an enemy by Satan, and he will do what he can to undermine our faith. Have you seen the forces of evil as they truly are? I have. I have seen entire communities so immersed and dependent on sin that Christians who resist the evil are despised and ridiculed. I have seen husbands and wives abused by angry spouses simply because of a desire that children know Jesus. I have seen those influenced by

Satan's purposes assume places of prominence among God's people and do everything in their power to divide and diminish Christ's church. But, perhaps worst of all, I have seen my cowardice in the face of what I fear Satan can do to me.

When God's people tremble before Satan, he wins. God tells us to be aware of Satan but not to fear him. Fear paralyzes us. Awareness arms us. We see the truth about Satan in God's Word, not on a movie screen, nor in the latest novel on the occult, even if it appears in Christian trappings. That same Word, which tells us the truth about Satan, also says we have nothing to fear if we resist him with the truths of God's care (see James 4:7; 1 Peter 5:9ff.). God promises that even if the evil of this world takes us as sheep to slaughter, nothing can separate us from the love of Jesus. Satan's reach always exceeds his grasp. He cannot conquer God nor defeat God's plans. We are to see the reality of Satan's attacks, but we are never to be blind to who is sure to win. Christ will be the ultimate victor of every spiritual war:

> And though this world with devils filled
> should threaten to undo us,
> We will not fear for God has willed
> his truth to triumph through us.
>
> Luther, "A Mighty Fortress"

The forces of this world may press me down, may hurt me, may steal my reputation, and at times may rob me of my joy or tempt me so that I fall. But I am yet in the hollow of God's hand. No one nor any thing can snatch me from his grasp. Christ will have dominion. He shows us his victories time after time if we will but see. Have you seen the power of God? I have. I have seen the lost saved. I have seen the embittered healed. I have seen the estranged reunited. I have seen God work and he is working still, because nothing in all creation can separate us from his love.

No Greater Love

On Sunday, August 16, 1987, Northwest Airlines Flight 225 crashed just after taking off from the Detroit airport. One hundred fifty-five people were killed. One survived: a four-year-old from Tempe, Arizona, named Cecelia.

News accounts say when rescuers found Cecelia they did not believe she had been on the plane. The crash was so devastating it did not seem anyone could survive. Investigators first assumed Cecelia had been a passenger in one of the cars on the highway onto which the airliner crashed. But when the passenger register for the flight was checked, there was Cecelia's name. As the crash investigators meticulously pieced together the details of the crash along with Cecelia's account, the mystery of her survival disappeared in the story of her mother's heroic care.

The reason, the experts say, Cecelia survived is that even as the plane was falling out of the air, Cecelia's mother, Paula Chichan, unbuckled her own seat belt, got down on her knees in front of her daughter, wrapped her arms and body around Cecelia, and then would not let her go.

Nothing could separate that child from her parent's love—not tragedy or disaster, not the fall or the flames that followed, not height or depth, not life or death. Such is the love of our Savior for us. He left his place in heaven's safety, lowered himself to us, and covered us with the sacrifice of his own body to save us. He will not let us go. Nothing can separate us from his love, not sin, nor circumstances, nor the flames of hell itself. The Bible assures us that neither death, nor life, nor angels, nor principalities, nor powers, nor things present, nor things to come, nor height, nor depth, nor any other thing in all creation

can separate us from the love of God that is in Christ Jesus
our Lord (vv. 38–39).

> Jesus loves me, this I know,
> For the Bible tells me so;
> Little ones to him belong,
> They are weak, but he is strong.
> Yes, Jesus loves me! Yes, Jesus loves me!
> Yes, Jesus loves me! The Bible tells me so!

QUESTIONS *for Thought*

1. Does God take all difficulties out of the lives of faithful Christians?
2. What are three ways God assures us in Romans 8 that difficult circumstances do not prove that his love has failed?
3. What are ways Satan may try to convince us that our relationship with God is broken?
4. What can separate us from the love of God?

ELEVEN

Snapshots of Mercy

Snapshots of the Gospel

A few generations ago preachers told the story of a man who decided to take his family to Colorado for a scenic vacation. To enjoy the modern conveniences of the era while taking in the scenery, the family went by train. After days of anticipation, the children got so excited as the first mountains came into distant view, their energy could hardly be contained in their small train cabin. The parents quickly decided a nap was needed to keep everyone from getting totally frazzled during the two hours it would actually take to reach the first range.

Everyone settled down to rest except the youngest daughter who was too excited to nap. In an attempt to keep her occupied (and keep her quiet) her father gave her a map to study the mountains they would soon cross. It was a bad idea. Only seconds after she began to examine the map, tracing her finger over the likely path the train would follow across the great mountains and valleys, the little girl let out a shriek. "Oh, Daddy," she cried, "we are going to fall off the mountains."

No matter how much the father tried to assure the girl that the train tracks were secure, the daughter could not be calmed. Her anxiety mounted as the train reached the first mountain and began to creep to higher altitudes. As the first peak came into sight her fright turned into a frenzy. She was convinced the train would fall off the other side of the mountain. Then the train reached the peak and the little girl squealed again, but this time her voice was filled with delight instead of fear. "Oh look, Daddy," she said pointing below. "Someone has gone ahead of us building bridges."

At last the father understood his little girl's worry. The mountains ahead appeared to be threatening precipices to the child who did not know the valleys had been spanned. She could not rest while this fear remained. But once she understood that someone had gone before her building bridges, she was stirred to new heights of appreciation for the splendor of the mountains. When her fears were allayed, she was filled with wonder at what had been provided for her. The climbing of each new peak added to her delight because of the encouragement she had found in the first bridge.

In the eighth chapter of Romans our heavenly Father has prepared a similar journey for us. He puts before us the map that traces the way to heaven. Great mountains must be spanned to get there. The holy standards of God stretch before us as an endless mountain range that must be crossed. Only a glance at the route will take our breath away, because we immediately recognize each mountain is separated from the next higher peak by an immense valley of human sin and weakness. The great gaps in our character and conduct that must be crossed on any journey to heaven seem insuperable. Our fretting over being required to make such a journey could know no rest had not Christ gone before us building bridges.

In this wonderful chapter of Romans, the apostle Paul introduces us to Christ and the work he has done. Paul speaks of a bridge in the shape of a cross that spans the mountains that would endanger our path to heaven. The cross marks the way our Savior went when he secured our way to God at the cost of his own blood. When we see the bridge that he has made, we recognize not only how hopeless would be our situation without him but how wonderful is our position because of him. With our route secured to heaven by Christ's work we are freed from fear of our own inabilities, stirred to delight in the path he has laid before us, and encouraged to continue the journey that he has mapped for our lives. As God intends, our pilgrimage becomes a delight to live because of the grace that alone makes the mountains passable and the journey possible.

Vacation reporting, like vacation travel, has matured since the days of train rides to the Rockies. Now, not only do we tell tales, we take pictures—lots of pictures. With this noble tradition in mind, it is time to take out a few snapshots of my own for your viewing at the end of this journey through the promises of Romans 8. My purpose is not merely to reminisce but to recapture key features of the journey, and to remind us where to return if we need to see such promises again. For, in its essence, this chapter of Romans is a snapshot of the panorama of grace displayed throughout Scripture so that each generation will tell the next the praiseworthy deeds of our God, his power, and the wonders he has done (Ps. 78). The bridges laid before us still exist. The one who laid them still works as carefully and maintains them as faithfully as he did for the first who believed. Their joy and strength can yet be ours as we see the beauty of the bridges they crossed.

Calmed by Grace

The first snapshot for you to view was taken only a few hours after our family returned from touring Colorado's Royal Gorge, one of the world's deepest canyons spanned by a suspension bridge. The picture is not of the gorge. Taken inside our hotel room, the photograph shows our younger son sleeping in his mother's arms. To understand the significance of this picture, you have to know our two boys.

The Adventurer

Colin and Jordan are very different. Colin, the older of the two, is a very deliberate thinker. He systematically analyzes everything. Jordan is the adventurer. A few weeks before our vacation their distinctive personalities were evident when we had our driveway paved for the first time. We adults thought we had the driveway paved for the sake of our car, but the kids knew instinctively that the real purpose of paving driveways is to provide a surface for roller skates. So with the new pavement came new roller skates.

When the boys put on their new roller skates their opposite personalities were demonstrated in classic form. Neither boy began skating on the new pavement. Colin started in the grass. He rolled down a gentle hill staring intently at the wheels to figure out how to turn and brake. He spent twenty minutes experimenting how to hold his arms and how to bend his body to gain the best balance and control.

Our second son also started out in the grass but headed for a different destination. He walked through the backyard to the swingset. Then he climbed to the top of the slide with the skates on, crouched in racing stance, and shouted, "Geronimo-o-o!" as he launched off for distant planets propelled by a wild, roller-skate slide. That is our Jordan "to a T," and that is also why the picture of him asleep in his mother's arms is so special to us. It captures a rare moment in this child's life.

The photo of Jordan looking so settled was all the more unusual because of the kind of day we had before the picture was made. We began with an early breakfast, played in the covered wagons of an old Western town, feasted on hot dogs and ice cream, shopped for Indian jewelry, visited Royal Gorge, and played in the fountains of a water theme park. While any one of these activities might wear out the average child, each one of them can be calculated to energize Jordan. Pack all these activities into one day and he is wound up so tight that even the slightest stimulus sends him bouncing into ever higher levels of orbit. When the time finally arrives for him to rest after such a day, it is no easy task to settle Jordan down. But my son has a wonderful mother, and she has discovered the secret of calming him when things seem on the verge of pandemonium.

Kathy takes Jordan into her arms and tells him about his birth. She says, "Oh, Jordan, when you were born we were so happy. You had red hair and looked just like your grandfather. Your father and I knew we would love you so much, and we knew nothing could ever take away our love for you. You used to talk to me with little baby sounds, and I would talk back to you even when I knew you didn't understand, just to tell you how special you were to me and how much I loved you. Your eyes were so blue that I almost never wanted you to sleep so I could keep looking at your beautiful eyes. Even when I got sick and had to go into the hospital right after you were born, I took you with me because I never wanted to be away from you."

When his mother tells him about his birth in such loving terms, Jordan becomes all ears. He listens so intently that he settles right down.

A Child of the King

Our heavenly Father deals as lovingly with us in Romans 8. Recognizing how events in our lives can make us anxious and agitated, he calms us with the truths of his own care. To settle us and allow us to rest in his love, the Lord takes us into his arms through these words and tells us again about our spiritual birth. He begins by affirming how special we will always be to him, saying, "There is now no condemnation to them who are in Christ Jesus." The reasons immediately follow (vv. 2–4). We are loved because God provided life for us through the sacrifice of his own Son. Christ Jesus made us "free from the law of sin and death." The guilt of our sin that keeps us from a living union with God, Christ Jesus took on himself when he died on the cross. Through the righteousness Jesus provides for us, we have spiritual life as we trust in him. We are born again. Just as all believers were once born physically, God now gives us spiritual birth. Not only does God provide this new life for us, he also explains it to us again and again in passages such as this to remind us by our birth of how special we are to him.

The importance of these continual reminders in Scripture of our spiritual birth must be understood. Believers can easily be as children who need to rest but cannot be calmed. Our circumstances, our sins, and our fears can keep our hearts in a constant state of agitation. We wonder if we are loved. We wonder if we have done enough, or too much. We wonder if God is worried about our worries, or distressed over the distance we feel from him. We find ourselves desperately needing his assurances but subject to doubts that clamor and will not let us rest. Cutting through the cacophony is the gentle voice of our Savior. Hands once pierced now stroke brows furrowed in distress; arms once outstretched in love's sacrifice now close in love's embrace; and the voice that commanded heaven's hosts to let our sovereign die now whispers our soul's relief. We can rest from our labors, rest from our wondering, rest from our doubting, and sink into the calm repose that is the assurance of his love.

In the assurance God offers is the spiritual rest that can calm and rejuvenate many believer's lives. Kathy and I have a wonderful friend who has been trying to help another Christian for several years. The young man who is the focus of our friend's attention is well known for being likable and goodhearted, but he does not have many close friends. Says our friend about this young man, "If he would just stop trying so hard to make sure people like him, his life would be so much easier." The young man cannot rest in his own acceptance. He is tormented by the worry that someone may not like him or that he has done something to offend another. As a result of his inability to accept the love offered to him, he ceaselessly strives to get attention and win the respect of others. He makes himself a nuisance, driving away any who would appreciate him. Because he cannot rest in the knowledge that the most important one in the universe has loved him with an eternal love, his relationships remain as transient as his self-confidence.

Two teens my family respects highly for their Christian testimony and maturity are from the same family. On several occasions we have tried to tell their mother how much we appreciate them, but she always thwarts our efforts.

We will say, "You have such wonderful kids, and our children have been so helped by them."

We have learned to anticipate her response. She will tell us some awful incident from one of her children's pasts and then assure us that the child is not all we believe, and she deserves no regard as a mother of such a child. It seems to bother her that she or her children would be well thought of. Something in her heart will not allow her to accept appreciation from others. As a result, her life is a constant battle against depression and self-inflicted misery. How we long at times to put our arms about her and crush God's love into her. We know that she will never be healthy, nor are her children likely to know their own worth, until she really knows she is a child of the king. Her birth was conceived in eternity, proclaimed by the angels, and secured by the Spirit. She is not required to make herself miserable to make herself acceptable to the God who gave her birth.

Too many of us know others like these two who have forgotten the beauty of their own birth. Successful men and women may ceaselessly chase happiness because they have not known the acceptance of their God. They rise to the tops of corporate ladders only to discover they are leaning against the wrong buildings or that someone has climbed them easier, faster, higher, or younger. They gain the positions they sought only to discover they do not have the respect they wanted. When they should be able to rest, they are no less driven to seek the esteem they increasingly find to be elusive or illusory. In their chase after self-fulfillment they bypass the spiritual answer offered by God to all who are held by him.

Our heavenly Father says, "I love you."

To prove it, he tells us over and over again of our birth. It is a story that can calm an anxious heart, heal a broken psyche, and make spiritually productive the most habitually driven father, mother, teacher, or friend.

In a believer's spiritual birth is the affirmation of God's acceptance. No scriptural truth is more important.

Nothing can make a person more important. The person whom God makes a child of the king of the universe can afford to rest from personal efforts to create importance or acceptance. Such a person already has more importance and acceptance than this world can offer. Could it be true of you? Yes, it can, and you will know it is so when you rest in his arms and read Romans 8 again. Listen to his voice as you read.

He says, "Oh, my child, when you were born by my Spirit you became precious to me. When I looked at you I saw my own Son in your eyes, and he is so beautiful to me. No one is closer to my own heart than he, and now that you are like him, no one is closer to my heart than you."

These are the words of birth that can let a child of God rest.

Stirred by Grace

Our next vacation snapshot captures my older son atop a huge Ferris wheel on Pikes Peak. When we took a trip to the Rockies, we ventured into this amusement park in Colorado Springs to give the kids a break from the long drive.

The Analyzer

Now remember, the son you see in this snapshot is "the analyzer." Everything requires explanation in detail for this child. He just is not going to do anything unless he knows how things work and how they will work out. For him to be atop a Ferris wheel near the top of Pikes Peak was worth capturing in a picture. He is such an analyzer, we rarely have the opportunity to see him taking such risks. What stirred him to make this venture? The assurance of his father's presence.

We had not been in the amusement park long before our boys had tried out all the kiddie rides, and "the adventurer," our younger son, began to look longingly at the big-kid rides. "Daddy, let's go!" he said. So, I asked the analyzer, "Do you want to go?" He thought about it for about fifteen seconds, weighing all the pluses and minuses. His brow furrowed, but it was obvious he was having difficulty coming to any conclusion, until he figured out the key variable for his equation. Then his face brightened and he asked the deciding question: "Daddy, will you go with us?"

I said, "Sure, I'll go with you."

He said, "Okay," and off we went.

We rode the Giant Swing, the Runaway Rocketship and even the Mindscramblin' Minetrain, but none of them prepared us for the Super Ferris Wheel. When the adventurer saw that great spinning wheel throwing bodies out into thin air atop that mountain, he squealed in glee and raced to the admission gate. The analyzer wanted to think about it a minute. He studied the gears in the drive mechanism, estimated the height of the highest car, calculated the velocity of the drop on the downward side, and still he had a question: "Daddy, are you gonna go with us?"

I said, "Sure, I'll go with you."

He said, "Okay, then, I'll go."

Colin was stirred to do what intimidated him, and what was in some ways beyond him, by the comforting assurance of his father's presence.

The Immanuel Principle

My son was able to attempt great things because of the certainty that the father who cared for him would be with him despite possible fear, hesitation, or failing. God stirs his children to greater heights of holiness and service in this chapter of Romans by assuring us of the same. He gives us courage to face the trials and tasks that challenge us by assuring us his love will always be with us. The apostle Paul writes:

Who shall separate us from the love of Christ? Shall trouble or hardship or persecution or famine or nakedness or danger or sword? As it is written:

"For your sake we face death all day long; we are considered as sheep to be slaughtered."

No, in all these things we are more than conquerors through him who loved us. For I am convinced that neither death nor life, neither angels nor demons, neither the present nor the future, nor any powers, neither height nor depth, nor anything else in all creation, will be able to separate us from the love of God that is in Christ Jesus our Lord (vv. 35–39).

With these words the apostle reminds us that our Lord's name is Immanuel (which means "God is with us") because that is our Lord's nature. The Immanuel principle permeates the pages of Scripture from the ancient prophets to future promises because God knows we are able to confront whatever challenges and intimidates us when we know our Father promises to be with us always (see Exod. 33:14; Isa. 7:14; Matt. 1:23; Heb. 13:5; Matt. 28:20). We can step forward confidently in the face of terrible trials and terrifying darkness, because our God goes with us. Nothing stirs us to action in God's behalf more than the certainty that nothing can separate us from him.

All will face trials that make a giant Ferris wheel seem like the child's play it is. Such challenges put our stomachs in our throats, panic our hearts, and confound our minds. We analyze the terror of those tomorrows, and in our dread ask, "Father, will you go with us?" In Romans 8 he answers, "Yes, my child, I will go with you. Nothing in all creation can separate me from you. I will go with you wherever life leads." His assurance lets each of us say, "All right, Father, because you are with me, I will go. As long as you are with me, I know I am okay."

These words do not always come easily to us. Challenges shake our confidence in God's presence. Difficulties send us spinning off our spiritual balance. We want to shut our eyes against what we dread, and in that darkness it is easy to lose sight of God, reel, and fall. But we need not fear the darkness nor fall if we remember our Lord's constancy. That which makes us want to close our eyes need not make us fall.

Consider how strange it is that you can keep your balance when you shampoo in the shower. There you are with your eyes closed, standing without support, flailing your hands through your hair and shaking your head like the wildest rock star. Yet, despite these frenzied gyrations, you keep your balance. What keeps you from falling? The water from the shower nozzle tapping you on your shoulder orients you. Though you may be oblivious to the effect, the presence of the stream of water helps you keep your equilibrium. You are able to stand in the darkness because of the reminder of where you are relative to the shower.

God enables us to stand in the darkest hours by reminding us of his constant presence. He just keeps tapping us on the shoulder. In his Word he reminds us of the stream of mercy that predestined his love before the world began and secures his love for all eternity (see vv. 29–30). In our world the splendor of his creation showers us with the message of the power that created this world and foreshadows a more glorious world to come (see vv. 18–23). Night after night the heavens pour forth speech about the greatness of our God, and there is no language in which they cannot be heard (Ps. 19). By their splendor the mountains also declare his praise (Ps. 148). The Word and the world combine to create our awareness of the constant stream of God's power and love that flows over us and keeps our feet under us.

But it is not merely from lofty mountains or starry heights that God speaks to us of his presence. In the person of his Son, our God himself walked among us. He broke bread with us. He suffered for us (Rom. 8:32). By his Spirit he still dwells with us (vv. 9–11) and strengthens us (vv. 12–16). Through his Son he still acts in our behalf (v. 34). Our God rightfully calls himself Immanuel not only because he once walked with men but because he remains with us in heart, presence, and purpose. We do not always understand our trials, but the cross reminds us of an infinite love that does not cease simply because the world does not make sense.

Nothing to Lose

Men and women are sometimes stirred to attempt great things when they are convinced they have nothing to lose. Christians may be such people not because they have arrived at a state of hopelessness but because they have acquired the assurance of God's presence. Knowing they cannot lose him, they can attempt amazing things for him. The greatest Christians in the workplace, in schools, in ministry, or in families are those who are stirred to confront the challenges before which their hearts would faint if they did not know that their Father went with them. You can be such a Christian when you recognize that, though you may risk everything for the sake of integrity, reconciliation, or testimony, you never risk losing your heavenly Father.

God is always with you. You will never face a trial that can deny your contact with him. You will never face an enemy that can deny your access to him. You cannot walk a path that God will not also travel when you seek him. You cannot lose his desire to support you. You cannot lose his willingness to forgive you. He is always embracing, ever encouraging, unceasingly building, and eternally loving. Nothing can separate you from him. Nothing should stir you more. Consider this day what God calls you to do, then do it because he goes with you.

Encouraged by Grace

The last snapshot of our journey features my three-year-old daughter, Cori. In the picture she sits in front of me while I try to sit tall in the saddle of a swaybacked trail horse named Sergeant. Cori is not happy. Her face is beet red and tears stream down her cheeks. She is not scared; she is mad. Her two older brothers sit on their own horses, and she cannot stand being treated like a baby who has to ride with Daddy. She could not have been more embarrassed and disappointed if we had tried to mount an infant's car seat on that horse and strapped her in.

One Day Sure

The only way I found I could calm Cori was to assure her that when she matures just a bit, she will be like her brothers. One day she will be able to sit on her own horse. Her day of glory will come. She has a future hope. Ultimately, Cori determined I was not teasing her. When she believed deep down in her three-year-old heart that what I was saying is true, she stopped her crying. Even though her world was not all she wanted it to be, she rode happily with me because she knew what was certain to come.

God knows we, his children, also need such a hope. Much in our world is not as we want it to be. Our weaknesses embarrass us. Trials plague us. The apparent accomplishments of others taunt us. Happiness seems as elusive as life's certainties, and contentment as tenuous as our successes. And yet as impossible as it sounds, the apostle Paul promises believers real joy in this world that can be so maddening. His encouragement is based upon our future hope. Paul says: "I consider that our present sufferings are not worth comparing with the glory that will be revealed in us" (v. 18). There is a better day to come. In that day of glory we will share a seat with our God, but it will bring us no shame (Rev. 3:21). We will sit on a throne of glory we have inherited by his grace (Rom. 8:17). Embarrassment and blame for weakness will fade with this world's trials as we rejoice in the full maturity God has planned for us before the earth's foundations were laid. Glory will one day be ours because God promises it. Deep belief in this sure promise is the certain hope that brings joy to this life that is so uncertain.

A Steady Hold

Our need for such an encouragement is confirmed by a candid recognition of how changeable this life is. It is astounding how quickly many things can happen. When we vacation now, we see more and more families with video camcorders. I read recently of a technical breakthrough that has led to a new product called a steadycam. The steadycam is a video camera that is supposed to compensate for the cameraperson's movement as the video is made. You recognize the need for such a camera when you get home from a vacation and try to watch a video of your kids on horseback which you took while riding a horse following. Because a camcorder is held in your hand, rather than steadied by tons of cement under studio floors that support conventional TV cameras, your vacation video jumps all over the screen. It is simply impossible for the hand to hold a standard video camera steady with all the changes the cameraperson and the camera subject are sure to experience. To compensate for the inevitable movement, technicians now have managed to put an adjusting mechanism in the steadycam that stabilizes the image. But the amount of adjusting needed to steady the camera's image astonished even the experts. No one anticipated how much things change in only a second of normal activity. To steady the recorded image the technicians discovered that their adjusting device had to compensate for changes every 250-thousandth of a second. More is happening, and more can happen, in any given moment on this earth than we can possibly imagine.

God does not pretend that our lives are without tragic insecurity in this changeable world (vv. 20–24). The degree of uncertainty we face could lead to despair were it not for the knowledge that God's hand holds us. Our lives and our hearts are steadied by his purposes and his promises. He has purposed to refine our image so that we reflect the likeness of his own Son (vv. 28–29). He has promised that none of the changes that we face in this life can distract him from this purpose or dissuade him from his care for us (vv. 35–39). We Christians may not star on video screens but we will shine in heaven, because God cannot be moved from his intent to glorify his children (v. 30).

The steadiness of God's character and affection encourage us when either our world or our sin threaten to shake our confidence of our relationship with him. When we would otherwise be tempted to cry out, "Oh Lord, your love cannot be real, because so much has disappointed me," the hope God provides as a result of his unchanging care keeps us from despair. The same is true when we cry from our knees, "Oh Lord, your love cannot remain, because I have disappointed you so much." Scriptural promise of God's unalterable affection grants the confidence we need to seek him again in repentance. Without fear of rejection, the heart yearns for confession whose darkest acknowledgments and most tearful expression only draw us more fully into God's embrace. Godly sorrow showers a withered spirit with heaven's favor.

When we believe the grace that holds us is stronger than our circumstances and our sin, then neither can counteract the weight of heaven's joy (see 2 Cor. 4:16–18). Such a perspective does not minimize the realities of the horrors we may face (or commit) here; it enables us to handle them biblically by accurately assessing the certainty of the glory that awaits us there.

The Strength of Assurance

The encouragement and strength available in the certainty of future love was well demonstrated to me by my father when I left home to go to college. As we made the five-hour drive from our home to the university, the uncertainty of what I was facing began to weigh on me. I was going to a campus I had never seen in a town I had never visited. My family and friends would be hours away. My high school standing and accomplishments would mean nothing in this new place. There was no assurance that I was not facing academics more rigorous than I could handle, temptations more powerful than I was prepared to resist, or loneliness more oppressive than I had ever known.

My father sensed my nervousness. At one point he pulled over to the side of the highway and stopped the car. Then he turned to look at me and said, "I want you always to remember what I am about to tell you. I don't know what will happen to you at this college, but you are my son and nothing is going to change that. You may fall flat on your face and think that you have disappointed your mother and me. Maybe we will be disappointed, but I doubt it. Still, even if I am wrong, you must never forget that no matter how badly you fail, no matter how bad things get, my home is your home. You are my son; I am your father. And nothing, nothing is going to change that."

I wish I could tell you that I never faced difficulties in college, but that would not be true. I faced some very hard things and some very bitter disappointments. But whenever the difficulties threatened to overwhelm me, my mind returned to that roadside conversation with my father and I found encouragement and strength for the matters at hand. The certainty of my father's affection and provision made the threat of any disappointment or failure I faced less intimidating and thus more controllable. I found strength in my father's assurances that no failure was greater than his love for me and no difficulty would deny his provision for me.

Our heavenly Father has had a similar conversation with every believer in this chapter of Romans. Here he pauses with us on our faith journey to tell us that despite the failures and difficulties we may face, his love is sure and our home with him is secure. That knowledge does not remove all the challenges from our lives, but it makes them manageable through the strength and encouragement his promises generate. Trust in the steadfastness of God's love and confidence in the certainty of our glory provide the reassurance our hearts need to serve him faithfully in this world of change and uncertainty.

The Promise of Grace

The sufficiency, constancy, and stability of God's grace provide the strength we believers need when we confront the challenges of difficulty or sin. With the rock-solid assurance of God's abiding care we are enabled both to confess our sin without sinking into despondency and to do his will without slipping into slavish fear. Gone is the cyclic hopelessness that results from trying endlessly to keep from sliding down the mountain of his favor. Departed is the angry despair that accompanies futile attempts to remove the burden of our guilt by frenzied deeds of contrition, which are never sufficient to satisfy an infinitely holy God. Replacing all human striving to grasp God is his promise to save us by his grace alone and secure us solely through the work of his Son. When we fully comprehend that his care for us is fixed and cannot be shaken, we serve God out of gratitude rather than guilt. Our effectiveness in kingdom service then trebles because we serve him without burdensome blame or paralyzing fear from which we have been set free. We stop questioning whether we love God rightly and begin rejoicing that he loves us eternally. The joy of the Lord becomes our strength. The service of the Lord becomes our delight as we exult in the wonder that he holds us despite our weakness.

The necessity and delight of depending on the God whose strength is beyond our own was demonstrated for me at the end of our vacation when my sons and I discovered we could play "helicopter" on the ceiling-scraping bunk beds in our cabin. The game is played when Dad lies down in the top bunk and hangs his arm over the side of the bed. Then as a child grasps that arm, Dad makes the noise of a helicopter and raises his arm to the ceiling—with child in tow for the ride. My older son was enjoying the game so much that his little brother had to give it a try. He grabbed onto my hand and started on the upward journey, but before his feet were six inches off the floor he yelled for me to stop.

"Daddy," he said, "you have to hold onto me. I can't hold onto you."

As I took his hand in mine to raise him skyward again, I recognized the poignancy of his predicament. My son wanted to reach heights higher than he could attain, but to do so he required his father to hold him. My child's grasp was too weak. The spiritual condition of the heavenly Father's children is the same. We are too weak to hold onto God. He calls us to heights of holiness far beyond us.

Our grasp is bound to fail if we rely on our own strength to maintain our hold on God. The message of grace in Romans 8 is as simple as our predicament is plain. Because we cannot hang onto God, he holds onto us. He promises us his love, his Son, his Spirit, his faithfulness, and his home. Like fingers on a divine fist closing over our own hands are the promises that secure us to our God. When that grasp is closed no one and nothing in all creation is able to pry it apart again (Rom. 8:38–39). We are lifted higher than we could ever reach. We are more secure than we could ever arrange. We are more loved than we can imagine.

When we cannot hang on, we yet abide in the promises of grace. In the grasp of our omnipotent God we find joy, peace, and strength. From these spring thanksgiving, confession, and service as we respond in gratitude, confidence, and love to the relationship God secures. God's promises annul Satan's threats and believers' fears. In divine safekeeping is the eternal comfort that generates spiritual enablement and holy zeal. Godliness thrives when God holds us in the promises of grace.

QUESTIONS *for Thought*

1. How can the story of your spiritual birth calm you when events make you anxious or agitated?
2. In what sense does your spiritual birth allow you to rest? How does your status as a child of God free you from the pursuit of self-acceptance and self-fulfillment?

3. How can the "Immanuel principle" stir a believer to step forward in acts of faith and to stay balanced in moments of darkness?

4. What can you not lose that can lead you to do whatever God requires and go wherever he calls?

5. How can the steadiness of God's grasp encourage you when facing your own weakness?

6. What can separate you from God's grace?

For Small Groups
or Sunday Schools

Discussion questions appear at the conclusion of each chapter of this book for those who may find it useful in small group or instructional settings, in addition to their own personal reading. Since small groups are increasingly discovering they can engage more persons in Bible study when they have resources enabling them to do in-depth study over six- to eight-week periods, the following schedule is suggested.

Week 1	Introduction
Week 2	Chapters 1 and 2
Week 3	Chapters 3 and 4
Week 4	Chapters 5 and 6
Week 5	Chapters 7 and 8
Week 6	Chapters 9 and 10
Week 7	Chapter 11

Those who would like to use the book through a traditional Sunday school quarter may find it helpful to use the following schedule:

Week 1	Introduction	Week 7	Chapter 6
Week 2	Chapter 1	Week 8	Chapter 7
Week 3	Chapter 2	Week 9	Chapter 8
Week 4	Chapter 3	Week 10	Chapter 9
Week 5	Chapter 4	Week 11	Chapter 10
Week 6	Chapter 5	Week 12	Chapter 11

Bryan Chapell has served since 1994 as the president of Covenant Theological Seminary in St. Louis, the national seminary of the Presbyterian Church in America (PCA). Raised in Memphis, Tennessee, Dr. Chapell pastored for approximately ten years in downstate Illinois before joining the faculty of Covenant Seminary in 1985 to teach preaching. He later served several years as dean of the faculty before his presidential appointment.

Dr. Chapell has served as a preacher and lecturer in churches, colleges, and seminaries throughout this country and abroad. He has also authored a number of books including: *Standing Your Ground: A Call to Courage in an Age of Compromise, Each for the Other: Marriage As It Is Meant to Be, The Wonder of It All,* and *Christ-Centered Preaching.* His most recent publication is *1 & 2 Timothy and Titus,* which he co-authored with R. Kent Hughes.

While pastoring his first church in Illinois, Dr. Chapell met his wife, Kathy. The Chapells have four children.